A Simple Guide to Mark

A Simple Guide to Mark

Paul J. McCarren, SJ

A SHEED & WARD BOOK

ROWMAN & LITTLEFIELD PUBLISHERS, INC.
Lanham • Boulder • New York • Toronto • Plymouth, UK

A Sheed & Ward Book

Published by Rowman & Littlefield Publishers, Inc.
A wholly owned subsidiary of The Rowman & Littlefield Publishing Group, Inc.
4501 Forbes Boulevard, Suite 200, Lanham, Maryland 20706
www.rowman.com

10 Thornbury Road, Plymouth PL6 7PY, United Kingdom

British Library Cataloguing in Publication Information Available

Library of Congress Cataloging-in-Publication Data

McCarren, Paul J., 1943–
A simple guide to Mark / Paul J. McCarren.
p. cm.
"A Sheed & Ward book."
Includes index.
ISBN 978-1-4422-1884-0 (cloth : alk. paper)—ISBN 978-1-4422-1885-7 (pbk. : alk. paper)—ISBN 978-1-4422-1886-4 (electronic)
1. Bible. N.T. Mark—Commentaries. I. Title.
BS2585.53.M385 2013
226.3'077—dc23
2012031727

Printed in the United States of America

Contents

Introduction: Why I Needed a Simple Guide to the Gospels

It took me a long time to hear what the Gospels say. Luckily, I spent much of that time with the Jesuits, an organization that is patient with slow learners. Like all the other religious orders in the Catholic Church, the Jesuits attempt to respond to Jesus' command in the Gospels to spread the Good News. So, Jesuits are required to take time learning what's proclaimed in the Good News. One method used in this learning process is the Spiritual Exercises of Ignatius Loyola. Most of those exercises are contemplations of Gospel scenes that are undertaken with the help of a director, just as physical exercises are often done with the help of a trainer. Jesuits go through these exercises at least twice. I did the Spiritual Exercises as a Jesuit novice; but when I did them again years later, I was shocked to discover I had no idea what I was doing.

The shock hit me late one afternoon as I read to my director a description of how the exercises had gone that day. As I read, he began to cough and clear his throat. He reached for a tissue and said, "Sorry; please excuse me. I've sometimes cried while listening to a write-up, but I've never laughed so hard." My look must have said, "What's so funny?" So he asked me to listen to what I'd been writing. After he read from notes he'd taken on my write-ups, he said, "Notice how you're picturing Jesus." I'd been imagining Jesus acting as a stern teacher who could barely control his impatience with people's slowness to understand his message. Over and over in my prayers I had seen Jesus as a man who was quick to find fault with the mistakes made by his followers. After asking me to notice that this image wasn't very appealing, my director reminded me that the Gospels describe someone quite different from the Jesus I'd imagined. They tell us, for instance, that many people found Jesus immensely attractive. Some of them even dropped everything to follow him. I had missed this simple fact. How was that possible?

At some point in my life I had slipped into the assumption that, because the Gospels describe a God who is infinite, it must be infinitely difficult to relate to him. The logic of that assumption seemed as obvious as the fact that because the theories of modern physics are extremely complex, physics is extremely difficult to get your mind around. But the Gospels aren't complex theoretical reflections on mysterious truths—and they can't be understood as such. They are four descriptions of how Jesus struggled to share his love of God with others, and how his struggle succeeded. The Gospel writers relate this success to us as simple Good News that Jesus invited others to enjoy and spread.

With the help of my retreat director, I stopped looking for hidden lessons in the Gospel narratives. When I began to reread the Gospels without the prejudice of my assumptions, it became clear that, despite many differences in the four texts, each evangelist's narrative zeroed in on the same thing: Jesus' passionate drive to teach by his words and his actions. Biblical scholars have pointed out that we don't know precisely how the Gospel texts reached the form in which they are now presented in the Bible. The Gospel of Luke glances at this fact when it begins with the note that accounts (yes, he says "accounts") had been handed down to the evangelist's generation by those who'd witnessed Jesus' ministry [Lk.1:2]. Then the evangelist promises to organize this material so that the reader might come to "realize the certainty of the teachings" [Lk.1:4]. All the Gospel authors (or, if you like, all the editors and copyists who arranged the work of the original authors into the various manuscripts from which our modern Bibles are translated) seem to share this purpose: to make it plain that Jesus taught about God's determination to bring his work of creation to glorious fulfillment in us, his children.

Years ago on retreat, when my director nudged me to take a careful look at precisely what the Gospels say, I began to see them as attempts to let readers hear what Jesus struggled to teach his first disciples to hear: good news. With my director's encouragement to note the simple facts and details set down by the evangelists, I began to feel that even someone as benighted as myself could begin to take in the Gospel's simple message.

WHY A SIMPLE GUIDE TO THE GOSPELS MIGHT HELP YOU

When I look back on my difficulty in noticing Jesus' simple proclamation of the Good News, I take comfort in the fact that my denseness isn't unique. For example, when Mark describes Jesus visiting Nazareth, his old neighbors are said to be so astonished by his teaching that they couldn't believe it. They ask, "Where did this man get all this?" [Mk.6:2]. What they heard seemed too good to be true, so they resolved the tension they felt between surprise and suspicion by choosing to be annoyed: "They took offense at him" [Mk.6:3]. Mark and the other evangelists relate such moments of rejection as dead ends—moments when the story they're telling comes to a temporary halt. In other scenes, however, doubt and astonishment don't end with a rejection of the Good News but lead to an awareness of its power to move the heart. For example, Luke describes the disciples' first response to seeing Jesus after his resurrection as a mix of bafflement and glee: "They were still incredulous for joy and were amazed" [Lk.24:41]. Here, the disciples' delight is said to be as real as their disbelief. A sense of befuddlement ("How can this be?") grips them even as they're filled with joy. One feeling doesn't cancel the other. Luke is telling us that doubts and suspicions needn't overwhelm us with dismay even when they're striking us with full force. What good news!

If you, like me (and like many disciples before us), have been confused by parts of the Gospel narratives, you too might benefit from some simple comments about each scene and event—such as my director's comment about the people who found Jesus fascinating. And you, like me, might be helped by noting that all of Jesus' followers had to grapple with his simple message before they could accept it. For instance, when the Gospel of Mark describes events after the resurrection, it portrays Jesus taking many disciples to task for their stubbornness: "He appeared to them and rebuked them for their unbelief and hardness of heart because they had not believed those who saw him after he had been raised" [Mk.16:14]. Recall, however, what Jesus says next to these slow learners: "He said to them, 'Go into the whole world and proclaim the Gospel to every creature'" [Mk.16:15]. Here Jesus entrusts the announcement of the Gospel—the Good News—to the very individuals who, when they first heard reports of the resurrection, couldn't believe them. It's natural to assume that, as these first disciples headed off to fulfill their commission to proclaim the Good News, they needed to review with one another what they thought the Good News was. They would have asked one another such questions as, "What was it he said that time we were caught in the storm; and what did we say in response?" As they recalled their various experiences of what Jesus had said and done, they would have helped one another review the recent past until they began to see a clear and communicable message—a message that others could grasp as Good News. In turn, those who heard this message began to write accounts of what they heard so still others could hear about Jesus and his struggle to proclaim God's truth as Good News. Each gospel proclaims this Good News, but each one proclaims it in a somewhat different way.

HOW IS MARK'S GOSPEL DIFFERENT FROM THE OTHERS?

Brevity: the Gospel according to Mark is the shortest of the four Gospels. Paradoxically, it's crammed with details missing in the other three. Most scholars agree that Mark's Gospel is the earliest of the four, and many suppose it was addressed to believers fearful of persecution, perhaps in Nero's Rome, perhaps in Galilee following the upheaval of the Jewish war against the Romans. It reads like an account by someone who is eager to grab the attention of distracted listeners. Its jam-packed brevity draws in the reader. The British actor Alec McCowen startled theater audiences in the 1970s and 1980s by delivering the King James Version of Mark's Gospel as a gripping story. His rendition of the Gospel made it clear that it's a series of vivid anecdotes (some frightening, some funny, some sad) that builds toward a surprising climax. McCowen showed that Mark's Gospel was composed by an author with a talent for moving the narrative forward swiftly—a guide in a hurry: "Look at this; and don't miss this; quickly now, look at this; next . . ." (Over the centuries, many commentators have supposed that the author of Mark's Gospel was the man named John Mark, a nephew of Paul's traveling companion, Barnabas, and an assistant to Paul—a relationship that soured [see Acts 15:37–38]. Even if this conjecture could be proved true, these biographical details add nothing to the fact that, whoever the author was, he felt he had an urgent message.)

Resistance: Mark's headlong style is suited to grabbing the attention of the distracted and fainthearted. One of his major themes also grabs attention: hostility. Mark peppers the reader with examples of puzzled or angry resistance to Jesus' message; he depicts even the disciples balking at Jesus' words. In Mark's telling, this strong resistance to Jesus builds relentlessly toward betrayal, death, and apparent defeat. This is a severe warning to believers. Mark seems to want them to realize that Jesus' teaching poses a demanding challenge to anyone attracted to it—and that many have been afraid to embrace it. For instance, the earliest manuscripts of Mark's Gospel end by describing the response of three disciples to an angel's instruction to tell other disciples that Jesus had been raised from the dead: "They fled from the tomb in a befuddled frenzy. They told no one anything because they were afraid" [Mk.16:8]—the end. This ending leaves the reader with the question, Is any worry keeping *you* from sharing this news?

Belief: the Gospel of Mark begins with the words, "The beginning of the Good News of Jesus Christ, Son of God." When this Gospel was read by someone unrolling a scroll, the end of the Good News would literally and physically be in the hands of that reader. The text could simply be rolled back up and passed on to another reader. Or it could be taken to heart. Mark seems to be saying, "What are you going to do with this news? Are you going to drop it as many have done before you, or will you become part of the story, and tell it to others?"

This is a brief list of some basic characteristics and themes of Mark's Gospel. The index lists a number of other key themes and directs you to the pages where you can learn more about them.

A TRANSLATION CHALLENGE

The Gospels were written in Greek. Many Gospel translations, including those in lectionaries used for formal church services, have been prepared by commissions of scholars. These translations not only render into English the words of the Greek text but also retain the original rhetorical phrasings. Because ancient Greek phrasing is different from modern English expression, a strictly literal translation is often hard to follow. The simplicity of an evangelist's message can escape us when a translation retains its original (and unfamiliar) turns of phrase.

In homiletic remarks, preachers often rephrase the text that's been proclaimed. They want to make sure we know what the text actually says before they comment on it. So, after a reading, they're likely to tell us, "What the evangelist is saying here is . . ." Like a preacher's careful rephrasing of a text, my translation of Mark's Gospel in this simple guide spells out anything that might be missed or muddled in a strictly literal translation of the original Greek words and phrases. The translation also includes occasional explanatory remarks that, in other translations, are relegated to footnotes or the accompanying commentary. I've put such explanations within the passages to let you keep reading Mark's Good News without having to stop to look up unfamiliar references.

ACKNOWLEDGMENTS

My comments after each section of my translation are derived from the study of many scripture commentaries. I am indebted in particular to the richness of the notes and commentary by John R. Donohue, SJ, and Daniel J. Harrington, SJ, published in the Sacra Pagina series of studies of the New Testament, and to the wealth of information in the notes and commentary of C. S. Mann, published as part of the Anchor Bible.

Many people encouraged me during the writing of the manuscript and helped me with comments on it. Thank you to Bridget Leonard, who worked long and hard as a literary agent for this work, and to Carole Sargent for her guidance at Georgetown University's Office of Scholarly and Literary Publication. And thank you to the parishioners at the parishes where I worked—especially to Dorothy Davis, Agnes Williams, Jayne Ikard, and to Tom and Mary Biddle. Other helpful comments came from my sister, Morgan, and from my friends Jean Reynolds and Alan Wynroth. I am grateful to my provincial superior of the Maryland Province of the Jesuits, who allowed me time to write this book, and to all my supportive Jesuit companions, especially James P. M. Walsh, SJ.

ONE

John the Baptist Proclaims Repentance and Forgiveness; Jesus Demonstrates Them

JOHN THE BAPTIST, WITNESS TO REPENTANCE [MK.1:1–8]

¹ *This is the beginning of the Good News of Jesus—the Christ, the Anointed one of God, the Son of God.* ² *First, recall Isaiah the prophet writing, "See? I send my messenger ahead, preparing your way." [Although Isaiah doesn't use this image of a "messenger" to describe how God made things ready for someone, the author of Exodus and the prophet Malachi do (see Ex.23:20; Mal.3:1). To see how Isaiah puts the same idea, go on to the next verse.]* ³ *[Isaiah writes:] "In the wilderness, a voice cries out, 'Prepare the way of the Lord. Make his pathway straight'" [Is.40:3].* ⁴ *In the wilderness, Baptizing John came out to proclaim a Baptism of Repentance, a baptism for the forgiveness of sins.* ⁵ *Into the wilderness went all of Judea, all in Jerusalem. All were being baptized by him in the Jordan, confessing their sins.* ⁶ *Clothed in camel's hair, with a leather belt around his waist, John fed on locusts and honey.* ⁷ *He proclaimed, "Someone more mighty than me is coming soon. Who? I'm unfit to stoop and fix the strap of his sandal.* ⁸ *I've been baptizing you with water. He'll baptize you with the Holy Spirit."*

The author of this Good News is like a modern reporter. He doesn't introduce himself or tell us how he tracked down this story. He simply begins to tell the reader what he knows, insisting he's about to unfold Good News, and that this is the beginning of it [v.1a]. The news is good because it's about a man, Jesus, who is God's anointed—that is, the one especially chosen to reveal the truth of scripture: the truth that God does reign in this world (see, e.g., Ps.89:20–29). And there's more: this Jesus is God's own Son [v.1b].

In his opening line, Mark assumes readers will recognize the title "the Christ"—Greek for "Anointed," which is "Messiah" in Hebrew. When he cites some of scripture's descriptions of God's actions, he seems to be saying, "You remember how God repeatedly promised to remind us of his care for us—of his presence with us. Recall the texts that encourage us to believe someone will always be calling us back to God—and recall that God himself promises to set the stage for his messengers" [vv.2–3]. Mark then says a man called "the Baptizer" fits the description of God's messenger. This messenger appeared where we might not expect much to happen—the wilderness. The messenger said people could be cleansed of all that corrupted them—they could be healed. He invited them to wash away their selfishness and turn to the God who made them [v.4]. Mark says people from all over responded to the Baptizer's proclamation; they admitted their selfishness and sought to be healed of it [v.5].

Mark seems concerned that we not mistake John the Baptist for a charlatan. He notes that John shows little concern for himself. He doesn't even care what he eats or wears [v.6]. Because he doesn't worry about his own needs, he's free to focus on what God wants— and what God wants, of course, is for people to hear about his concern for them. So John proclaims the nearness of God [v.7]: "The mighty one is coming!" Perhaps because everyone knows how difficult it is to trust a promise—because we prefer a bird that's in the hand to two that are in a bush—Mark tells us the Baptist told his audience why they might want to wait for the one who was coming. What if, he said, you had more than water with which to cleanse yourselves of selfishness? What if your mean-spirited selfishness—

your sinfulness—could be replaced by the Spirit of God? Look forward to that [v.8].

JESUS IS DRAWN TO BAPTISM, REPENTANCE, AND TEACHING [MK.1:9–20]

⁹ What happened next was this: Jesus came down from Nazareth, in Galilean territory, and was baptized in the Jordan by John. ¹⁰ As soon as he came out of the water, he saw the heavens break open. He saw the Spirit plummeting to him like a dove. ¹¹ From the heavens came a voice: "You are my Son. I love you. You are my delight." ¹² As soon as that happened, the Spirit urged Jesus into the wilderness. ¹³ He spent forty days there—tempted by Satan; circled by beasts; attended by angels. ¹⁴ Then, after the imprisonment of John the Baptizer, Jesus went up to Galilee to proclaim the good news of the kingdom of God. ¹⁵ [He was saying:] "The time for the kingdom of God is now. Turn, and put your faith in this Good News." ¹⁶ Now, walking along the Sea of Galilee, Jesus saw Simon and his brother Andrew, fishermen casting nets into the sea. ¹⁷ He said, "Come with me, and I'll make you into fishers of souls." ¹⁸ They left their nets at once, and followed him. ¹⁹ Going along farther, he saw James, Zebedee's son, and his brother John. They were in their boat mending nets. ²⁰ Right then he called them. They left their father, Zebedee, with the hirelings, and followed after him.

Jesus enters Mark's account of the Good News suddenly, as if drawn by John's celebration of baptism [v.9]. Mark doesn't offer a motive for Jesus' action, but he does describe its result. There's an unusual movement in the sky that suggests a theophany, and the Spirit, of which John just spoke [v.8], breaks upon Jesus with the suddenness of a dove diving home [v.10]. Then Jesus is addressed from heaven with words that could only come from a doting parent [v.11]. All this happened because Jesus sought baptism. He was recognized by God—"my Son"—because he turned to God in a ritual that proclaimed: "I wash away all that I am—I am dead to myself. I am now filled with your divine life." We're beginning to see what Mark meant when he called Jesus "Son of God" in his opening statement (see v.1). For one thing, it means that Jesus is completely reconciled to accepting the life the Father gives him.

Inspired by the Spirit, Jesus' first decision was to enter the wilderness to be tempted [v.12]. For those who think of temptation as the brief moment before we do something stupid, this might seem like a puzzling decision. In this case, however, following as it does Jesus' decision to be baptized, it's an opportunity to savor the pleasures of that decision. In other words, after choosing to turn to God and finding the choice delightful, Jesus spent forty days repeating his choice: "Should I turn to myself? No; it's more enjoyable to turn to God." This is a basic and simple form of prayer. It's the sort of praying offered by the Psalms, for instance, "Happy the one who turns from evil ideas . . . but delights in the law of the Lord" (Ps.1:1a, 2a). Although Jesus is described without any human contact or comfort, and is pictured with only wild animals for company, we're told he experienced the ministering care of God [v.13].

Mark then quickly changes the scene. Perhaps because the imprisonment of the Baptist suggests danger in Judea, Jesus moves north to Galilee. But he doesn't hide there. He proclaims the Good News [v.14]—news of what he himself experienced in the wilderness: the kingdom of God. Yes, the promise God made in the Covenant to be our God, and to care for us always, is being fulfilled now. So repent—let go of all self-concern. Turn to God for care [v.15].

The first response to Jesus' proclamation is depicted as swift and unhesitating. Though Mark describes Jesus' invitation to the fishermen without any explanation of himself or his message, we don't have to assume they had no idea who Jesus was. These four businessmen, supposedly having heard something of this man's proclamation of the Good News, jumped at his invitation to join him in sharing this Good News with others [vv.16–20].

JESUS TEACHES AND HEALS [MK.1:21–28]

[21] *Jesus and his new followers went to Capernaum. On a Sabbath, he went into the synagogue and taught.* [22] *They were amazed at his teaching. He spoke with*

authority—not like the scribes. ²³ *Suddenly, a bedeviled man started to yell:* ²⁴ *"You, Jesus, the Nazarene, what's this to you? Are you trying to destroy us? I know you. 'Blessed-by-God'!"* ²⁵ *Jesus cut in, "Stop! Come out of him."* ²⁶ *The bedeviling spirit contorted the man, made a loud noise, and left.* ²⁷ *Everyone was dumbfounded. They started to chatter: "What's this?" "It's a new teaching!" "A lesson with real force!" "Unclean spirits listen to it and obey!"* ²⁸ *This news about him traveled all over the countryside [of Galilee].*

———◦◦◦———

Mark describes Jesus immediately showing his disciples how he taught. He went into a city, found its assembly place, and proclaimed: "The kingdom is at hand; turn to it" (see 1:15; v.21); and the audience was amazed. Mark lets us know Jesus didn't impress his hearers because he was saying something new, but because he was saying it as they'd never heard it before [v.22].

According to Mark, Jesus' message of repentance was met by a demonic protest [v.23]. If we find it hard to believe in demonic possession, we might ask if we ever react to ideas defensively. New ideas can confuse and baffle us; shocking news can upset us. Here, a man experiences Jesus' powerful presentation of his message as a threat: "Why is this Jesus from Nazareth destroying my preconceptions with his teaching? I know! He thinks he's specially sent by God" [v.24]. Mark didn't need to be a psychiatrist to know that some people are overwhelmed by obsessions—are bedeviled by a need to cling to their convictions. This is the sort of bedevilment he describes here.

Jesus' response to the man's severe reaction to fresh ideas is described simply and succinctly: "Be still. Let all distress go" [v.25]. After a short struggle and a loud protest, the bedeviled man let go of his spirit of distress, and it disappeared [v.26]. This action confirmed the assembly's first impression: Jesus spoke powerfully and acted powerfully—even bringing peace to a man in tumult [v.27]. This sounds like very good news. So they spread it [v.28].

JESUS TEACHES AGAIN THROUGH HEALING [MK.1:29–45]

²⁹ Jesus left the synagogue and went home with Simon and Andrew; James and John along with them. ³⁰ Simon's mother-in-law was down with a fever, which they mentioned to Jesus. ³¹ When Jesus went over to her, he took her hand and helped her up. The fever left her, and she attended to them. ³² After sunset, they brought to him anyone with an illness, as well as anyone who was bedeviled. ³³ The whole city was at the door. ³⁴ He healed many from all sorts of diseases. He cast out many demons, but kept them from saying what they knew about him. ³⁵ [Next morning,] when it was still dark, he got up, and went off alone to pray. ³⁶ Simon and the others went looking for him. ³⁷ They found him and said, "Everyone's looking for you." ³⁸ "Let's go around to nearby towns," he said, "to make my proclamation there. That's why I've come." ³⁹ And he made his proclamation in synagogues all over Galilee, casting out demons [as he went].

⁴⁰ And up comes a leper begging him on his knees, "If you want to, you can make me clean." ⁴¹ Overwhelmed with pity, Jesus put out his hand, touched the man, and said, "I do want to. Be clean." ⁴² He was instantly clean—completely cured. ⁴³ With a kind of growl, Jesus sent the man's evil spirit away. ⁴⁴ Then he said, "Now look, don't go talking about this. Instead, go present yourself to the priest and offer the cleansing sacrifice [described in the opening verses of Leviticus 14] as it was set down by Moses. That will certify to all that you are clean." ⁴⁵ But he went out and started saying all sorts of things and spreading the word around, so that Jesus could no longer just walk into a town. He had to stay in open country—where they came to him from all over!

——◦◦◦——

A visit to the home of Simon and Andrew reveals that the lady of the house is sick—a condition that was quickly noticed, and quickly attended to [vv.29–31]. This event is over almost before we take it in. With a few details, Mark succinctly shows us Jesus' instinctive impulse to bring comfort and healing. The disciples' natural response to the illness was to say, "Mother's sick." Just as naturally, Jesus' inclination was to approach the sick person, trusting that the person could be made well.

Next, the simple house visit becomes a citywide event [vv.32–33]. All Capernaum seems to have heard of the healing of the bedeviled man (see above, vv.27–28). But what exactly had they heard? Although Jesus is described responding to their needs—healing the sick and freeing folks from their demons—he's also described forbidding the demons to speak [v.34]. Mark doesn't explain the injunction, but it seems Jesus was determined to speak for himself. He didn't want the Good News to be distorted by the bedeviled man in the synagogue (see 1:25), and he doesn't want it twisted here. Perhaps to indicate what Jesus does want, Mark describes him practicing what he's been preaching: Jesus goes aside to pray—he turns to God [v.35].

When Mark says the disciples told Jesus everyone wanted him, he doesn't say what they wanted [vv.36–37]. But he does tell us what Jesus wanted: to continue proclaiming his message that, because God's kingdom is here, people should accept it [v.38]. So he moved about in Galilee, preaching in synagogues. And when he encountered hurts that hindered repentance, he healed them [v.39].

Mark then describes Jesus' healing touch in response to a leper begging for help [vv.40–41]. If we think, "Of course Jesus is so moved by this man's need that he reaches out to him," we should notice how quickly we've accepted Mark's depiction of Jesus as someone whose overwhelming desire is to free others from burdens so they might hear the Good News [vv.41–42]. Verse 43 might be translated: "Groaning, he got rid of him." Are we to think that Jesus was dismissing the leper, or some bedeviling spirit? True, the leper hasn't been described as bedeviled by a demon. But Jesus' words here suggest he assumed the man needed to be freed from an oppressive spirit. So he freed him [v.43] and then told him that, because he'd been freed from sickness and anxiety, he could be at peace—that is, he need not boast about his newfound serenity [v.44a]. All he needed was to obtain official recognition from the community's representative that he was indeed well [v.44b].

But Mark says the man did tell everyone his story. It wasn't Jesus' story, of course. Jesus' story is about nothing more than the thrill of hearing and sharing the Good News—the Good News of turning to the God who is bringing us into the kingdom (see 1:15). According to Mark, the healed leper's publicizing of his good fortune stirred up such general excitement that Jesus had difficulty getting a hearing in other towns for his specific message: repentance. Even when Jesus withdrew, people came out from the towns to find him [v.45]. (Did they go out to hear the Good News?)

TWO

We Turn to God because God Answers Our Needs

RETURNING TO CAPERNAUM, JESUS FORGIVES AND HEALS
[MK.2:1–12]

¹ When Jesus later returned to Capernaum, word got out that he was back home. ² So many gathered, no one could get through the door. He spoke the word to them. ³ Four men were approaching carrying a paralyzed man to him. ⁴ Since they couldn't get close because of the crowd, they took off some roofing on his house and lowered the paralytic, in his mat, through the opening. ⁵ Jesus saw their faith. So he says to the man with the paralysis, "My son, your sins are forgiven." ⁶ Some scribes sitting there muttered in their hearts. ⁷ "Why does he say this?" "He's blaspheming." "Who but God forgives sin?" ⁸ Jesus right away felt in his soul their inner debate. "Why are you chewing this matter over in your hearts?" he asked. ⁹ "What's easier to say to this man: 'Your sins are forgiven'; or 'Stand up, take your mat, and go'? ¹⁰ Let's help you understand that the Son of Man has the ability on earth to forgive sins." He turned to the paralyzed man and said: ¹¹ "I tell you to stand. Pick up your mat. Go to your home." ¹² He got right up. He picked up his mat. He left the house for all to see. Everyone was amazed. They gave glory to God. "We've never seen the like," they said.

Mark describes Jesus leaving Galilee, and returning to Capernaum—making himself at home, presumably, in the household of
Simon and Andrew [v.1]—where crowds again seek him out. His
response to their presence is to teach them [v.2], proclaiming, we
suppose, the same message Mark says he proclaimed at first: "Turn
to the kingdom, now!" (see 1:15).

It's not been clear from Mark's descriptions that people understood this proclamation of reconciliation with God. Some certainly
turned to Jesus for healing of physical distress. But aside from the
protest of a departing demon (see 1:24), no one has yet spoken
about spiritual healing. In this scene, Mark says the four men and
their paralyzed friend wanted to "get close" to Jesus. He doesn't say
they sought a cure, but neither does he say they sought anything
else [vv.3–4]. It's Jesus who's pictured expanding the notion of what
it means to seek healing: he mentions faith [v.5a]. Then he says what
he means by faith—namely, that you can trust in God's forgiveness
[v.5b]. His statement about forgiveness is completely consistent
with his teaching: because God's kingdom is at hand, you can repent from whatever has preoccupied you, turn to the kingdom, and
be reconciled with God.

Scribes were official interpreters of scripture, and would know
that scripture describes God as merciful and forgiving (see, e.g., the
opening of Psalm 32, 51, or 85). But here they appear dumbfounded
by Jesus' statement [v.6]. It seemed blasphemous to them to say sins
were forgiven because it was an encroachment on a divine preroga-
tive [v.7]. Jesus was puzzled by their reaction [v.8]. He seemed to
think they should know how easy it was to forgive. Surely they
understood that forgiveness and spiritual well-being were easier to
get than physical health [v.9]. If not, Jesus would help them understand. Learn, he says, that a human being, a "Son of Man," has the
power to celebrate and share God's forgiveness right now—to repent and enjoy the kingdom right now [v.10]. Then he freed the
man from paralysis and told him to use his new freedom to walk
home [v.11]. The man went home, freed from both sin and paralysis; and the crowd's amazement provoked them to offer praise and
thanksgiving to God [v.12]. In other words, they impulsively did

what Jesus had been encouraging them to do. They turned to God, whose presence, or kingdom, suddenly seemed quite real. What Good News.

The scene ends on a happy, almost triumphant note. But during it, Mark also introduces the Gospel's first clear signs of trouble. Not only does he highlight a fact that might not have been obvious previously—namely, that people were more interested in Jesus' power to heal than in his message of repentance—but he also discloses a new and unsettling fact. Some scribes, who might be expected to preach the same message Jesus was preaching, didn't seem to understand repentance, reconciliation, and forgiveness. It seems that some Jewish teachers weren't encouraging people to seek the astonishing joy and comfort of God's mercy.

A CALL TO A SINNER; AN ARGUMENT ABOUT RELIGIOUS PRACTICE [MK.2:13–22]

[13] Jesus left the center of Capernaum and went down to the lake [of Galilee]. The crowd followed him, so he continued to teach them. [14] As he moved along, he saw Levi, son of Alphaeus, collecting taxes. He said, "Follow me"; and he got up from his tax collecting and followed him. [15] Later, he reclined at table in Levi's house—with many tax collectors and other sinners joining them, along with the disciples, and many hangers-on. [16] Scribes from the Pharisee sect saw sinners and tax collectors at the table. They asked Jesus' followers why he ate with sinners. [17] Hearing this Jesus says, "The hearty don't need a healer; the sick do. I don't appeal to the self-righteous, but to sinners. [18] [Soon after that,] Jesus was questioned by people who knew that the disciples of John the Baptist and of the Pharisees practiced fasting. They asked, "Why do those disciples fast, but yours don't?" [19] Jesus said, "Do the bridegroom's attendants fast while they're with him [at the wedding]? They can't fast while the groom's with them! [20] Later, when the bridegroom is taken away, there will be time for them to fast. [21] No one would sew a fresh patch of cloth on an old garment. The fresh patch would shrink, pull away from the hole, and make it worse. [22] And no one would put fresh wine in an old wineskin. The wineskin would burst—ruining both wine and wineskin. New wine is put into new wineskins."

———◊◊◊———

From the beginning, Mark has described Jesus' words and actions prompting strong responses. Jesus' first invitation to follow him was leapt at [1:18]. He was mobbed after his first cure [1:28, 33], hotly pursued during his visit to the Galilean countryside [1:45], and sought out by many on his return to Capernaum [2:2]. In this scene, crowds are once again attracted to him. He walks along the shore, and the whole town joins his stroll. We're probably not surprised to hear Mark say that Jesus took this opportunity to continue to teach the Good News [v.13].

Mark then tells us that Jesus noticed a tax collector busy at his job. Jesus' instruction to Levi to follow him couldn't be more succinct—nor could Levi's response [v.14]. This is another of Mark's examples of the attractiveness of Jesus' bold message: "Turn from your present fixations and follow me to the divine kingdom!" And it was followed by the pleasure of a big meal, enjoyed by all the wrong sort of people, where one can assume Jesus again took the opportunity to proclaim his Good News of reconciliation with God [v.15].

But once again Mark depicts the scribes (the people who knew the rules derived from scripture) insisting that Jesus was breaking the rules. Anyone can sympathize with their question: why does Jesus eat with sinners [v.16]? Why does he associate with people who, by legal definition, are outside the religious community? (Would people speak favorably about someone in their neighborhood who invited a busload of felons to lunch?) Jesus' answer was simple: his call to turn from sin makes sense only to sinners [v.17]. If it wasn't already clear to us, this scene should make it obvious that Jesus' one desire is to proclaim the Good News of reconciliation, healing, and forgiveness (see 1:15).

Mark tells us some people wondered why Jesus' disciples didn't observe traditional religious practices—why, if Jesus' followers wanted to turn to God, they didn't fast as a sign of their repentance [v.18]. Jesus is described explaining that, if you're rejoicing in the Good News, it makes no sense to fast—any more than you'd celebrate a wedding by abstaining from the wedding feast [v.19]. However, if your source of joy disappeared, that would be the proper moment to curtail your eating. Why? Fasting could remind you that you need something more than food [v.20]. Yes, food is necessary. But for true life, we need to be nourished by Jesus' teaching about repentance. If that lesson is lost, so is your life.

As if to insist that Jesus is serious about this bold image, Mark describes him explaining the importance of learning anew what you think you already know. If you piece together your ideas thoughtlessly, your thinking will be in tatters, like clothing carelessly patched [v.21]. Just as you can only add to your store of wine if you find the right container for a new vintage, you must clear your mind of stale ideas if you want fresh insights [v.22]. Mark portrays Jesus telling his questioners that, if they truly want to be knowledgeable about religious practices, they won't resist new ideas. Rather, they'll examine how these new ideas might strengthen the practices they already know.

ANOTHER ARGUMENT ABOUT RELIGIOUS PRACTICE
[MK.2:23–28]

²³ Once, on a Sabbath, Jesus was walking through grain fields. As the disciples with him went along, they plucked the grains. ²⁴ The Pharisees complained, "Look! Why are they doing that? That's not allowed on the Sabbath." ²⁵ He asked, "Haven't you read what David did when he and his companions were hungry and needed food? ²⁶ Remember how he went into the house of God, during the high priesthood of Abiathar, and ate the presentation loaves [the special Sabbath bread prescribed by Law (Lev.24:5–8)]. He did this, and shared the bread with his men, even though the Law says it's to be consumed only by the priests." ²⁷ He then said, "The Sabbath was created for us human beings, not the other way around. ²⁸ The Son of Man is Lord of all creation—even the Sabbath."

———*᷑ʋᴥ*———

Mark describes a natural reaction to walking through tall grass: tugging on the tops. But the disciples' action disturbs the Pharisees, strict observers of the Law [vv.23–24]. Mark says Jesus responded to their accusation with a question: are they sure they understand the scripture that underlies the Law [v.25]? For example, surely they remember the story, from the First Book of Samuel (1 Sam.21:2–7), whose lesson is that human needs are answered, not overruled, by divine laws [v.26].

Jesus is described as patient with the Pharisees. Because they were a lay group that followed the Law strictly, he expected them to know the commandments—the Covenant described in Exodus (Ex.20:1–17). In the first three commandments, God's people are directed to entrust themselves completely to God's care. The remaining commandments tell people to treat one another with respect—honoring parents, offending no one, even avoiding envious thoughts about others. Later in this Gospel, Mark will describe Jesus summing up the Covenant as love of God and love of one another (see below, 12:31–32). That summary emphasizes what the commandments already say: if you accept God's care for yourself, you'll respect God's care for everyone else—you'll see no difference between you and your neighbor. The Sabbath celebrates this Covenant with God. It's a weekly reminder to rejoice in his gift of creation—to enjoy what the author of the Book of Genesis describes as our lordship over the earth (see Gen.1:28). We humans, "sons of man," are to act together as responsible lords of creation [vv.27–28].

THREE

Who Needs Forgiveness, Healing, and Wholeness?

ANOTHER DISAGREEMENT ABOUT HEALING [MK.3:1–6]

[1] *[On another Sabbath,] Jesus went to the synagogue. A man was there with a withered hand.* [2] *[Some Pharisees] watched to see if he'd heal him; then they could charge him with doing so on the Sabbath.* [3] *He says to the man with the withered hand, "Stand in the center."* [4] *Then, to the Pharisees he says, "On the Sabbath, is it allowed by the Law to do good, or to do evil—to save life, or destroy it?" They said nothing.* [5] *Looking at them, Jesus felt deep anger and sadness because of their hard hearts. So, he says to the man, "Unfold your hand." He unfolded it. The hand was restored.* [6] *The Pharisees left and went straightaway to the associates of Herod—the Herodians. Together, they plotted Jesus' destruction.*

Mark again describes Jesus in a synagogue on a Sabbath, where Jesus noticed a man in the assembly who had a crippled hand [v.1]. The Greek text doesn't identify the spies in the scene as Pharisees at first, but names them later in the narrative. Some members of this religious movement were directly challenged by Jesus about their interpretation of Sabbath Law (see above, 2:25–28); now, in turn,

15

they seem eager to challenge the way Jesus observes—or, in their view, violates—the Sabbath [v.2]. Mark depicts Jesus responding to their spying by addressing the reason for the weekly gathering: "What are we celebrating on the Sabbath? Are we celebrating the gift of life God gave us, or not?" But these Pharisees refuse to have a discussion—even though the Pharisaic movement was dedicated to the study of the Law [vv.3–4]. So, Jesus is stymied. He can't teach those who don't want to learn—he's overwhelmed by the frustration and sadness of meeting unmovable hearts [v.5].

We don't know who made up the group referred to by Mark as "Herodians." But the basic point here is that some individuals in Capernaum and its environs were not only unmoved by Jesus' proclamation of the Good News, they also felt that its message of reconciliation, forgiveness, and healing should be silenced. They felt threatened or affronted by Jesus' teaching, so they began to organize a lethal opposition to Jesus and his impulse to bring physical healing to those who needed it [v.6].

MANY SEEK HEALING; JESUS ASKS DISCIPLES TO HEAL
[MK.3:7–19]

[7] Jesus went with his disciples to the shore of the lake. Great numbers followed him. They were from Galilee and Judea. [8] They were from Jerusalem and Idumean territory [farther south]. They were from the other side of the Jordan, and from Tyre and Sidon [in the northwest]. [9] He asked his disciples to keep a boat ready in case the crowd pushed too close. [10] Since he'd healed so many, they were crushing one another as they pressed forward with their afflictions to touch him. [11] If any with unclean spirits saw him, they fell, crying, "You're the Son of God." [12] He put them abruptly in their place—not wanting them for heralds. [13] Up then he goes to the mountain and calls for those he wanted to come to him, and they came. [14] He designated twelve as his counterparts—calling them "apostles" ["those sent"]. He appointed them to proclaim [the same message he proclaimed]. [15] He gave them the power to drive out demons. [16] The twelve he designated were: Simon, whom he called Peter; [17] James and his brother John, sons of Zebedee, whom he called "Boanerges" ("Sons of Thunder"); [18] Andrew;

and Philip; and Bartholomew; and Matthew; and Thomas; and James, the son of Alphaeus; and Thaddeus; and Simon, "the Zealous"; [19] and Judas Iscariot, who betrayed him.

————◦/◦/◦————

Mark has told us that those who disapproved of Jesus' healing were plotting against him. But this menace doesn't change Jesus' behavior; he continues to heal [v.10]. And people are attracted to him from many places [v.8], in great numbers [v.9], even when he leaves Capernaum [v.7]. Mark has told us that Jesus' behavior put him in danger. But he hasn't described Jesus as anxious. He's portrayed a man insisting on the message he wishes to convey—a man who doesn't let troubled souls cry out their version of truth. He's a man whose actions will reveal that he is the Son of God—a truth already proclaimed by the Father (see 1:11). Mark says Jesus didn't want competing voices as he continued to reveal his message [vv.11–12]. He wanted followers who would speak with his voice. Notice that Mark doesn't say Jesus wanted his spokesmen to speak about him. Instead, they are to proclaim his message: God's kingdom is at hand, and it brings healing to those who need it [vv.13–15]. The personal histories of those whom Jesus sent are obviously not important to Mark. Otherwise, he would have reported them. His list reveals only that Jesus shared his work with twelve close followers who were ordinary people with various characteristics—including a readiness to abandon the mission and betray the one who sent them to fulfill it [vv.16–19].

CONFUSION ABOUT HEALING; EXPLANATION OF HEALING AND FORGIVENESS [MK.3:20–30]

[20] *Back home [in Capernaum], another crowd gathered. Jesus and his disciples couldn't find a moment to break bread. [21] When his family heard about this, they decided to restrain him since he seemed out of his mind. [22] Some scribes had come from Jerusalem [i.e., teachers, belonging to the Pharisee movement, who'd already been plotting against him (see above, 2:6, 16; 3:6)]. They said,*

"He's got the Spirit of Deceit, Beelzebub. He can get rid of demons because he's controlled by their demon-leader!" [23] *Jesus asked for everyone's attention. Then he offered some parables. "How can Satan, the leader of demons, get rid of himself?* [24] *If a kingdom's split into factions, it won't survive.* [25] *If a household splits, it won't survive.* [26] *So, if Satan challenged himself—splitting himself up— that would be the end of him.* [27] *You can't rob the well-defended unless you disable them; then you can haul away!* [28] *O, yes indeed, let me tell you, all will be forgiven—yes, all the sins of turning away from God, and all the nonsense you speak about God!* [29] *However, if you say you reject the divine Spirit, how can you receive divine forgiveness? You're choosing the sin of turning away from God forever—never to feel forgiveness."* [30] *He spoke these parables because they'd said, "He's got the deceitful spirit."*

——⦿⦿⦿——

It seems that, whether Jesus is in a house in Capernaum, or down by the Lake of Galilee, needy people gather, and he responds to their needs. To do this, he even neglected his own needs [v.20]—a choice his family considered mad [v.21]. The healer was judged unwell for wanting to heal—a judgment also made by Jesus' opponents. They said he was possessed [v.22].

Mark then describes Jesus trying to help his opponents reimagine their assumptions. They should ask: if he were evil, would he work against evil [vv.23–27]? What, then, was he doing? He was doing this: asking them to notice what their desires and intentions were—to reconsider things. He's saying, of course it's easy to get depressed and give up on God—turning away from the Covenant and its promises, refusing to trust that God can perfect creation. But all our bitter fussing and fuming against God's ways is forgiven when we turn back to him [v.28]. However, if we insist on ignoring him, following only our way of seeking and getting what we think is good for us, we're sentencing ourselves to a miserable state. Or, put quite simply, if we won't let ourselves be touched by God's Spirit, we obviously condemn ourselves to living without that Spirit [v.29]. Mark says Jesus shared these images with his opponents to point out the foolishness of their thinking [v.30].

JESUS' WORRIED FAMILY APPEARS [MK.3:31–35]

³¹ Jesus' mother and brothers come to his house in Capernaum and, kept outside because of the crowd, send in word to him. ³² The crowd hunched all around him starts saying, "Look, your mother's here!" "Your family's here—your brothers and sisters!" "They're outside." "They want you!" ³³ So he says, "Who's my mother? Who are my brothers?" ³⁴ He looked at all those crowded around and said, "See? My mother; my brothers! ³⁵ Whoever does what God wants is my mother, my brother, my sister."

—⟡⟡⟡—

After referring to Jesus' anxious relatives (see above, v.21), Mark brings them on the scene [v.31]—an arrival that provokes commotion. Those jamming Jesus' door and taking up his time quickly defer to something more pressing than their ills—relatives! Suddenly, nothing's more important than Jesus' family. Think of your playground days, when, though you were in the middle of an important game, someone says, "Your mom's calling you!" It trumps all other calls [v.32].

But not this time. Jesus is described asking the desperately polite crowd to reconsider their most cherished beliefs. Do we, he asks, truly know who is "our own"? Who are they [v.33]? Is it possible to see others, even in their worst need, as more intimately connected to us than our own family [v.34]? The answer for Jesus is yes.

Mark doesn't spell out here what Jesus meant by the words "what God wants" [v.35]. But God's will has been described repeatedly from the beginning of this Gospel. God's desire for a smooth and easy access to us was cited by Mark from Isaiah as practically his first word (see 1:2–3). And the evangelist has repeatedly described Jesus proclaiming the presence of God's kingdom—along with the message that God wants us to turn and accept his gift of the kingdom. Here Jesus is portrayed challenging his listeners to ask themselves: "When I'm in need, do I turn to the God who wants to answer all my needs? Do I want what God wants? Do I want to let God get to me?" If your answer is yes, then Jesus sees you as his closest relative.

FOUR

How Does God Get at Us?

A GIFT OF PLENTY [MK.4:1–9]

¹ Another time, a large crowd gathered around Jesus as he taught by the lake. This time he got into a boat and sat out on the lake—with the crowd standing on the shore. ² He used parables to teach. This is how he taught them. ³ "Listen to this," he said. "You see, there was a sower who went out to sow. ⁴ As he sowed, some seed fell along the road, and birds ate it. ⁵ Some fell on hard, rocky soil. Lacking any depth, it pushed right up. ⁶ But, when the sun beat down, it shriveled for lack of a root. ⁷ Some fell down among the thistles. And when the thistles shot up, they choked it off. No grain grew. ⁸ Some fell on good soil. It rose up, grew, and bore grain—one spot thirtyfold; another, sixty; yet another, a hundredfold. ⁹ If your ears hear, hear!"

The previous time Mark described crowds following Jesus to the shore, he said Jesus had a boat ready, but didn't use it (see 3:9). Here, if we imagine an even larger crowd, we can see that Jesus might need a boat from which to be (safely) seen and heard [v.1]. Then, says Mark, he used parables to teach [v.2]. A parable sometimes states a comparison outright—"the kingdom of heaven is like a mustard seed." Here, however, Jesus is portrayed describing the

21

fate of sown seed, but not saying to what the fate of the seed should be compared [vv.3–9]. This parable may therefore seem like a riddle: "Guess what the sowing-and-growing process is like." The answer may seem obvious to anyone who's already heard the story. But if we imagine the people in this scene as similar to those in previous crowds, we'll see them as desperate for healing miracles. How would a story about grain interest them?

We can suppose it didn't interest them much, and that they asked themselves, "Why has he brought up planting?" On the other hand, they could just as well have said, "I'm not sure what the seed's compared to here, but I certainly get the point that it can be amazingly fruitful." In other words, it's clear that natural and easy abundance is the point of the story. What might come to the minds of believing persons when they hear about the blessings of plenty?

THE GIFT OF PLENTY EXPLAINED [MK.4:10–20]

¹⁰ Later, away from the crowd, those around Jesus with the twelve asked him the meaning of his parable. ¹¹ He said, "All that's unspoken about God's kingdom has been given to you. But everything [about the kingdom] comes in parables to those outside it. ¹² In this way [of learning repentance that Isaiah also described], 'they may look and look, but not see; listen and listen, but not catch it—lest they repent, and be forgiven' [Is.6:9]." ¹³ Jesus asked, "Didn't you grasp this parable? Then, how will you understand all the other parables? ¹⁴ The sower is sowing the word. ¹⁵ The word that falls by the way hits those who, as soon as it strikes them, are tricked out of it by Satan. ¹⁶ In the rocky places, they take in the word with joy, ¹⁷ but, because they don't let it root, it passes away. When troubles come or someone pesters them about the word, they drop it, and it's lost. ¹⁸ Those among the thistles have heard the sown word. ¹⁹ Then the preoccupations of this life— such as obsession with money and yearning for things—stifle the word. It comes to nothing. ²⁰ Those on good soil are those who hear the word, take it in, and bear its fruits—some, thirty; some, sixty; some, a hundredfold."

—◦◦◦—

According to Mark, it's not some member of the crowd who requests an explanation of the above parable; it was one of Jesus' followers. They hadn't caught the obvious point that God's presence, once accepted, works mightily and richly in us [v.10]. Jesus' response to their request is ironic, but not dismissive. His intention, it seems clear, is to teach; and if his hearers can take a little ribbing about their obtuseness, they'll learn from their ignorance. Jesus reminds his followers that he's been repeatedly proclaiming a truth about the kingdom that may have previously seemed mysterious—that is, not clearly expressed [v.11a]. He's told anyone who will listen that the kingdom is here. It's now; and it can be embraced now. Those who haven't grasped this erstwhile mystery will need to learn it through examples and parables [v.11b].

Mark describes Jesus reminding his disciples of Isaiah's description of how the Lord explains the process of repentance: your blindness and deafness must become so dire that you can no longer ignore your condition. Only when you're overwhelmed by your weakness (your self-centeredness, your sin) will you turn and get help—that is, forgiveness [v.12].

The question that Mark says Jesus asked next added another touch of sarcasm. If they'd been thinking they already understood his teaching about the kingdom, but now realized (from their need to ask him to explain the parable) that they didn't understand him—that is, if they felt left out of the conversation (see v.11)—what did the realization of their ignorance tell them? Readers will understand that it tells them they still have much to learn. What more appropriate need could a disciple or a student have than the need for more learning?

So Jesus continues their lessons. We hear him tell them to compare the result of the sower's work with the result of God's work. From the beginning of creation, God has been at work making and fulfilling promises to us, his children. Despite this divine effort, we keep finding the same reasons for resisting his work—paying little attention to God's word or refusing to give it time to grow. We're so busy caring for ourselves that we don't take time to imagine someone else might do a better job [vv.14–19]. However, if we did let our

lives flourish into what God wants to make of them, we'd be astonished at the richness of results [v.20].

MORE LESSONS ABOUT LEARNING [MK.4:21–25]

*²¹ [Jesus continued to teach his followers.] "Do you bring out a lamp to put it
under a bushel-size basket, or under the bed," he asked; "or, do you put it on the
lamp stand? ²² Just so, nothing is hidden except to be brought out; nothing kept
secret that's not uncovered. ²³ If your ears hear, hear!" ²⁴ And he said, "Savor
what you hear. Do you pay more attention, or less? If you pay more, you'll hear
more! ²⁵ Do you take things in? Then you'll keep getting more. If you don't take
hold of things you won't even keep what you've got."*

———⟨⟩———

Mark doesn't mention a change of scene, so we can imagine Jesus
still inside his house talking to his close followers. He's described
entertaining them with a children's lesson: "Where do you put a
candle—in the straw?" "No!" "Where then—under the blanket?"
"No!" "Should it go on the table?" "Yes!" Toddlers might laugh at
such a lesson while grasping the truth that things are only useful in
their proper places. The disciples are relearning the importance of
this lesson [v.21]. Jesus applies this lesson—everything in its place
and a place for everything—to patient listening. If you're certain
something doesn't fit, or doesn't make sense, listen again. Even
things that at first seem obscure or strange will eventually spill their
secrets [v.22]. Pay attention to what I'm saying, their teacher tells
them [v.23].

The lesson continues with a repetition of the main theme—listen!—and a reminder that listening takes work. Only if you deliber-
ately pay attention, only if you take in and mull over what your
senses pick up, will you keep being enlightened [v.24]. As a matter
of fact, if you don't eagerly open up to what's being revealed to
you—if you don't pay attention to the world around you and to the
God who created your world—you'll lose whatever grip on life you
think you already have [v.25].

LESSONS ABOUT THE KINGDOM — IN PARABLES [MK.4:26–34]

[26] [Continuing to teach his followers,] Jesus said, "This is what the kingdom of God is like. One day, a man throws seed on the earth. [27] He goes to sleep. He gets up. This goes on day after day. Meanwhile, the seed would be sprouting and growing—he has no idea how. [28] Earth brings the seed to fruition all by itself: from grass, to buds, to grains of wheat. [29] After it ripens, you reach for a scythe—the harvest has arrived. [30] Now, let's see; what else could we compare God's kingdom to—what's another parable for it?" said Jesus. [31] "It's like a mustard seed. When it's planted, it's the smallest thing on the ground. [32] But after it's sown, it grows taller than all the other plants in the garden. Its branches offer the birds of the sky nests in the shade." [33] With many similar parables, he kept speaking his word to them—as many stories as they could take in. [34] He didn't speak without using parables. But when he was with just his disciples, he spelled things out.

———∽∾∽———

From the beginning, Mark has described Jesus proclaiming God's kingdom (see 1:15). Jesus repeats this proclamation, heals the unwell, and tells people to turn away from sin to accept the kingdom. Here, he teaches how to accept the kingdom, saying we can accept it as we accept plant growth: it happens unseen and without our help — though we reap its benefits [vv.26–29]. We might also accept the kingdom the way we accept the fact that something as seemingly insignificant as one tiny, dry seed can evolve into a large shrub whose leafy canopy creates a complicated ecosystem [vv.30–32].

Jesus, says Mark, was a tireless teacher who taught by telling stories [v.33]. Yes, he repeats, it was important to Jesus to feed people's imaginations with stories [v.34a]. He wasn't a philosopher offering a theory of life, or a guru outlining a method for self-improvement. He was instructing others how to imagine God at work. Mark also tells us what we're about to see for ourselves as this Gospel unfolds: when Jesus is away from the big crowds and talking with only his close followers, he can have longer conversations, during which he can speak more fully [v.34b] — as he did, for instance, after the story about the various fates of seeds (see above, 4:13–20). After all, if they're truly going to learn from him, they'll have to develop a deep appreciation of his words—making them their own.

A LESSON IN TRUST [MK.4:35–41]

[35] Near the end of another day spent with his disciples, Jesus said, "Let's cross the lake." [36] So, they left the crowd that had gathered around him and, without further ado, got him into a boat. Other boats followed along. [37] A terrific wind came up and battered his boat with waves, almost swamping it. [38] He was in the stern, sleeping on a boat cushion. They woke him up and said, "Teacher, don't you care we're going to die?" [39] He got up. He cut the wind off. He said to the lake, "Ssh. Lie still." The wind died. It was calm. [40] "Why the fear?" he asked. "Where's your faith?" [41] They drew back in great anxiety. "Who is this person," they wondered. "He makes wind and water do what he wants!"

—⟨⟩⟨⟩⟨⟩—

Earlier, Mark said Jesus wanted to preach throughout Galilee (see 1:38–39). Here, Jesus has the impulse to bring his message across the Lake of Galilee [vv.35–36]—to what's referred to as "Gerasene territory" (see below, 5:1). Then a life-threatening storm hits. But Mark depicts Jesus as unmoved by the danger, and he describes Jesus' tranquility as a shock to his followers—evidence to them that he didn't care that they were going to die [vv.37–38]. The disciples' consternation at the fact that Jesus doesn't seem to worry about death may seem ironic to those who know the Gospel. Of course Jesus isn't worried about death. Dying is part of the life God has designed for us—part of the kingdom that Jesus is proclaiming.

Jesus' actions, as Mark describes them in response to his disciples' appeal, may seem like the work of a wizard. In fact, that's the reaction Mark seems to attribute to the disciples (see v.41). But it can also be seen as a lesson in dealing with fear. Are the disciples afraid of what the world can do to them? Watch, says Jesus; it can do nothing to you [v.39].

It can do nothing, that is, if you've put your trust in something greater than your own defenses against the unpredictable forces of this world [v.40]. Mark doesn't tell us whether or not the disciples grasped this lesson. But the description of their stupefaction suggests they still had much to learn [v.41]. They're a long way from realizing that, just as the Sabbath was made for them (see 2:27), so were all the works and ways of creation—including dangerous waves and death.

FIVE

Two Healings Provoke a Desire to Testify

[1] They landed on the other shore—the territory of the Gerasenes [in the Decapolis, bordering the southeast side of the Lake of Galilee]. [2] As soon as Jesus got out of the boat, a man with an unclean spirit came out of the burial chambers [on the cliff] and approached him. [3] The man haunted the chambers, and couldn't be kept safe, even with chains. [4] People had often tried to tie him down, using iron bonds, fetters, and chains. But he broke the bonds and smashed the chains. [5] All day and throughout the night, he wandered the burial chambers and the cliffs, bellowing, and bruising himself with rocks. [6] Sighting Jesus from the heights, he ran to him and fell before him. [7] "What's this to you?" he shouted. "Jesus, son of the Most High God, by that God, I beg you to leave me alone"—[8] because Jesus kept saying, "Get out of him, unclean spirit." [9] Then he asked, "What's your name?" "My name is Legion," he said; "we're many." [10] And the man kept begging repeatedly that Jesus not send them out of the territory.

⸻ ⁓⁓⁓ ⸻

For students of geography, Mark's setting of this scene will make little sense. But he's telling a story, not composing an atlas, and the details he sets down are all we need to follow the plot. First, says Mark, after the eventful boat ride with his disciples (see 4:37ff.), Jesus landed in Gentile territory [v.1]. If we've assumed Jesus wanted to proclaim his message only in Galilee (see 1:38), we should recall that his deeds have drawn people from all over the map (see 3:8).

Mark says Jesus' first encounter in Gentile territory was with a man so distressed and bedeviled in spirit that he avoided all who sought to keep him from his self-destructive behavior. He howled in pain with only corpses to keep him company [vv.2–5]. Mark tells us this man was drawn instantly to Jesus, but then begged to be left alone; he was a heart in conflict [vv.6–7]. Like the bedeviled man healed in the synagogue (see 1:24–26), this tortured soul, says Mark, spoke of Jesus' closeness to God—here, calling him God's son [v.7a]. Readers might be thinking, "Well, demons would know that sort of thing." Such thinking, of course, assumes that no mere mortal could recognize a close relationship with God in someone else. But this man, cut off from all human contact and comfort, sees Jesus as someone blessed by divine peace. And why not? When we're anxious, don't we envy the composure of others? This man apparently saw in Jesus a peacefulness he identified as a familiar bond with God—a bond quite different from his own bondage to fear and despair. And yet Mark tells us the man refused to imagine what it would be like to be freed from enslavement to delusions and to be, like Jesus, a child of God. Instead, he asked Jesus not to give him the pain of choosing to be reconciled to God [v.7b]. What a sad state of confusion.

Jesus, on the other hand, is described as quite calm and focused. First, he tells the demon to leave the man alone [v.8]. Next, after encountering resistance, he enters into conversation with the demonic spirit: "Tell me about yourself" [v.9a], to which, says Mark, the bedeviling presence answers, "I'm not just one, but many" [v.9b]. Then Mark describes the evil force presenting the sort of deal a child would come up with when a parent is about to throw out a tattered security blanket: "No, don't throw it away. Just put it up in the closet. I promise I won't touch it. Please!"

Although modern readers might think Mark has described this man's bedeviling spirit with primitive oversimplification, a fundamental truth about human fear and distress is captured in his portrayal of the man's anxious request: even though we may have a legion of disturbing anxieties, we may not want to let them go [v.10].

THE HEALING ACROSS THE LAKE CONTINUES [MK.5:11–20]

^11 On the heights above the cliffs, a large herd of pigs was grubbing for food. ^12 The man's demons pleaded with Jesus, "Send us into the pigs. Let us stay there." ^13 He let them go. The unclean spirits left the man and entered the pigs. Then the herd bolted down the cliffs into the lake. About two thousand of them drowned there. ^14 The swineherds ran off and spread this news in the nearby city and all over the countryside. People gathered to see what had happened. ^15 As they edged toward Jesus, they saw the man who'd been possessed—sitting down, clothed, sound of mind. This was the one bedeviled by a legion! They were frightened. ^16 Eyewitnesses told the new arrivals what had happened to the man and to the pigs. ^17 People started pleading with Jesus to leave their territory. ^18 Then, as he was getting back in the boat, the man who'd been possessed pleaded to be allowed to stay with him. ^19 Jesus said, No. Then he said, "Go home to those you know. Tell them all the Lord has done for you. Tell them he showed you mercy." ^20 The man went off and began to proclaim throughout the territory of the Ten Hellenistic Cities [the Decapolis] all Jesus did for him. People were flabbergasted.

—————◊◊◊—————

The entrance of pigs into this story emphasizes that we're in Gentile territory—where people didn't follow the Jewish rule of avoiding pigs [v.11]. Mark describes the demons as so desperate to lurk in their familiar neighborhood that they were willing to infest animals [v.12]. Jesus lets the demons go, but the dismissal turns out to be final. The man and the countryside are freed from the unclean spirits [v.13]. Anyone worried about the local economy might not see this as good news [v.14]. But Jesus' proclamation of the Good News shouldn't be confused with a politician's promise to make the world a better place. Mark doesn't describe Jesus as a reformer, but as a teacher who tells his listeners to seek healing and wholeness—gifts that are visible in the man who's no longer possessed. The crowd, however, didn't share the man's newfound peace. They were full of fear [v.15].

Mark reports that the worried locals wanted to go about their business without help from Jesus. They asked him to go [vv.16–17]. They could see the serenity of the man restored to health, but they seemed to fear that such a peace-filled life was achieved only through the loss of something they treasured. They were right. Mark has described Jesus telling people to turn to God's kingdom for fulfillment. Neither demons nor a thriving pig business can fulfill our deepest desires and needs.

Mark doesn't describe Jesus inviting the healed man to follow him as a disciple (see 1:17–20). But he reports that the man nonetheless wanted to go along with him [v.18]. He describes Jesus proposing a different idea that amounted to this: "I came here thinking I might proclaim my message of repentance, healing, and forgiveness. Now I ask you to proclaim it for me" [v.19]. So, says Mark, the man not only told his story to the people he knew, he traveled and preached the Good News throughout the entire Gentile territory of the Ten Cities; and he startled his hearers wherever he went [v.20]. We read earlier that Jesus appointed twelve of his disciples to preach the Good News and free people from their demons (see 3:14–15), but we haven't yet seen them fulfilling their commission—for that, see below (6:12–13). Here, without much fanfare, Mark tells us that one lone soul, in response to Jesus' request that he tell his story, unsettled the assumptions of a whole region. By telling his story and describing God's kindness to him, he challenged many others to seek satisfaction in something other than themselves.

RETURN TO GALILEE; MORE PLEAS FOR HEALING
[MK.5:21–34]

21 Jesus sailed to the other side of the lake [returning to Galilean territory]. Such a large crowd gathered that it kept him down by the shore. 22 Up comes Jairus, a synagogue leader. Sighting Jesus, he kneels before him. 23 He pleads, "My daughter is about to die. If you just place your hand on her, she'll find healing. All will be well." 24 Off Jesus went with him. And the large crowd followed, pushing on all sides. 25 But along came a woman who'd been suffering from a blood flux for a dozen years. 26 She'd undergone useless treatments from doctors—spending all and getting nothing. In fact, she was worse. 27 She'd heard of Jesus. So she joined the crowd and went up and touched his tunic. 28 She thought, "If I can just touch part of his clothes, I'll be healed." 29 Instantly, her blood problems disappeared, and she could tell she'd been healed.

30 And instantly Jesus could feel that his power had been tapped. He looked around the crowd and asked, "Who touched my clothes?" 31 "With such a crowd," said the disciples, "you ask who touched you?" 32 But he kept looking around for the one who touched him. 33 The woman was shaking with dread. But, because she knew what had happened, she came up, collapsed in front of him, and poured out the truth. 34 "Daughter," he said, "it's your faith that heals you. Go in peace, and enjoy being healed."

———✤———

Mark told us earlier that news of Jesus' presence spread quickly (see 1:45). Here again, as Jesus lands somewhere in Galilee, Mark describes crowds gathering [v.21] and a synagogue leader making an appeal [v.22], evidence that Mark doesn't depict all Jewish officials reacting negatively to Jesus. Jairus' request is portrayed not only as a parent's need, but also as a trust that Jesus had the power to restore life merely by laying on his hands [v.23]. The pushing crowd's close pursuit of Jairus and Jesus suggests they were curious to know how Jesus was going to help Jairus [v.24].

As Mark describes it, trust in Jesus' healing power—not curiosity—was what moved a woman suffering from vaginal bleeding. Like Jairus, she believed that one touch would bring healing. But, says Mark, she believed Jesus didn't need to initiate the touch. Simple contact would be enough [vv.25–28]. As Mark tells it, she was right; swiping a hem, a fold, or a sleeve made her well [v.29]. And why not? Jesus has been described as moved by others' needs not because the needs themselves were pitiful, but because needy individuals had sought help. Jesus has been described being moved by expressions of need. (See, e.g., the first three healing stories: a bedeviled soul cries out in a synagogue [1:24]; the disciples point out Peter's ill mother-in-law [1:30]; and a leper asks to be made clean [1:40].) Jesus is instinctively attracted to those who are hungry to hear the Good News that reconciliation—healing—is now.

Although Mark says Jesus was surprised by the sensation of power [v.30a], he doesn't portray that power as a mystifying divine energy radiating in all directions, striking anyone lucky enough to get within its range. Earlier in this Gospel, in the scene of Jesus' baptism, Mark described Jesus' power by saying that his confession of complete dependence on God moved his Father to boast of his delight in their relationship (see 1:10–11). In other words, Jesus' power is his ability—his need, his wish, his longing—to put himself into his Father's hands. His power is divine power because he does nothing to impede God's work in him. He also senses in others their longing for God—even before he's quite caught sight of it [v.30]. Mark says his disciples were baffled (perhaps annoyed) by Jesus' desire to know who had sought to share his power. They make fun of what seemed like a ridiculous request: to find in the crowd the one needy person whose touch was different from the general scuffle [v.31].

But Mark tells us Jesus wanted to put a face on the silent grab for help [v.32]. We can imagine the woman's embarrassment at both the intimate nature of her illness and her bold reaching for the gift of a cure. Nonetheless, we hear that she confessed her neediness [v.33], and that Jesus told her how she found divine healing: because she turned to God in desperation and put her trust in him, she found kindness, comfort, and peace—that is, healing [v.34]. This is the same lesson Jesus hoped the crowd would learn when they heard him tell the paralyzed man that his faith brought him forgiveness (see 2:5).

This lesson may have been difficult to grasp. What's the difference between desperately seeking solace, and desperately seeking solace from God? Mark has described Jesus answering this question with one word: faith. Faith works quite simply. For instance, if you had complete confidence that your doctor could free you from an illness, arranging for treatment would be cause for celebration. Similarly, if we trusted that God meant to bring us peace and contentment by bringing his kingdom to fulfillment within us, then turning to him would be delightful.

JAIRUS' DAUGHTER [MK.5:35–43]

[35] *As he was talking to the woman who'd been healed, people came up to the synagogue leader from his household. They said, "Your daughter died.* [36] *Why bother the teacher now?" Jesus overheard them and said to the synagogue leader, "Don't fear. Just believe."* [37] *He wouldn't let the crowd follow—except Peter, James, and James' brother, John.* [38] *They get to the man's house and find confusion, tears, and howling.* [39] *He asks, "Why the uproar and tears? The child hasn't died. She's asleep."* [40] *They laugh at him; but he shoos them out, and goes with the child's father and mother, and his disciples, into the room with the child.* [41] *Taking the child's hand, he says, "Talitha koum." That means, "Little one, I tell you, rise up."* [42] *Immediately, the little girl arose and started to wander about—she was just twelve. They were all beside themselves with amazement.* [43] *He told them emphatically that no one should know of this. And he said they should give her something to eat.*

———ⁿⁿⁿ———

By entwining two healing stories, Mark repeats a message: in hopeless situations (e.g., a woman is sick for years; a little girl is reported dead) Jesus is attracted to those who are willing to trust and believe [vv.35–36]. When Mark describes Jesus asking the crowd to hang back [v.37], we may suppose he was being sensitive to the synagogue leader's grief, or that he didn't think the crowd would

understand that the mourners' assumption could be wrong
[vv.38–39].

According to Mark, just as the disciples thought no one could
identify one needy supplicant in a roiling crowd (see above, 5:31),
these mourners see Jesus' assurances as risible. But Mark says Jesus
continued to be moved by the father's trust and wasn't distracted
by the mourners' lack of it [v.40]. "Rise," we hear him tell the girl
[v.41]—a command we will all hear when we die. Mark tells us the
girl accepted Jesus' invitation to rise, but her mother, father, and the
disciples didn't know what to think [v.42]. So they were given a
simple task: feed the girl [v.43b]. Mark told us Jesus asked one man
(whom he'd freed from a legion of demons) to tell others about his
healing (see 5:19). Here he tells us Jesus asked the witnesses to this
rising from what appeared to be death not to tell what they'd witnessed [v.43a]. Mark creates the impression that Jesus may have
thought that, unlike the Gentile who let go of his devils, these pious
Jews weren't yet ready to proclaim the Good News of healing and
reconciliation.

SIX

Incidents of Rejection; More Examples of Care and Healing

JESUS GETS A POOR RECEPTION AT HOME [MK.6:1–6]

¹ Jesus left that Galilean sea town and traveled to his home town, Nazareth. His disciples went with him. ² When the Sabbath came, he taught in the synagogue. Many who heard him were stunned. They said, "Where did he learn all this?" "How did this one get wisdom?" "What about his powerful works?" ³ [And they asked,] "Isn't this the carpenter—Mary's son, and the brother of James, and Joses, and Judas, and Simon? Don't his sisters live here with us?" They couldn't get over him. ⁴ He said, "A prophet isn't ridiculed—except by his neighbors, by his relatives, and in his home." ⁵ He could do no powerful works there, although he healed a few sick people by the laying on of his hands. ⁶ He was surprised and puzzled by their unbelief. He went to other towns to teach.

Earlier, Mark said Jesus wanted to proclaim the kingdom in many towns (see 1:38). So we're not surprised to hear he traveled to Nazareth [v.1] and taught on the Sabbath. We've seen that one Sabbath assembly was impressed by his words (see 1:21–22); and another was infiltrated by wary officials (see 3:1–2). In this scene, Mark tells us Jesus' neighbors were certain he couldn't be as learned as he

37

seemed or as powerful as they'd heard. They not only refused to believe what they'd heard, but also to ignore their own senses [vv.2–3]. They seem unable to imagine that God's promise to care for them could be manifested and fulfilled in so familiar a figure as their old neighbor, Jesus. (Note that Mark's main point here is not to offer a quick sketch of Jesus' extended family, but to observe that the people of Jesus' hometown weren't prepared to hear anything new from him—not even Good News.)

Mark says Jesus cited the truism—and joke—that you can't impress those who knew you as a child. But at the heart of the joke is a sad fact: we cling to our prejudices. Reconciliation and healing are impossible for anyone whose assumptions go unexamined. In this instance, only a few individuals sought healing and received it [v.5]. Jesus has seen hardness of heart before (see 3:5), but Mark depicts him as distressed to encounter it again—even among his friends and neighbors [v.6].

JESUS SHARES HIS MISSION WITH THE TWELVE; HEROD IS PUZZLED [MK.6:7–16]

7 Jesus then sent his disciples to teach. Calling the twelve together [somewhere near Capernaum], he sent them off in twos, giving them control over unclean spirits. 8 He told them to take with them only a walking stick—no food, no sack, no coins. 9 They could have sandals, but not two tunics. 10 He said, "In whatever house you stay, remain until you depart. 11 If they don't welcome you or listen to you, leave. Shake off the dust from your feet as your witness to them." 12 So, they went off and proclaimed repentance. 13 They cast out many demons. They anointed many sick with oil and healed them.

14 As reports of Jesus' name and work spread, Herod noticed. Some were saying, "John the Baptist is raised from the dead and now does powerful works." 15 Others said, "It's Elijah [returned to restore our kingdom (see Sir.48:10)]." Others said, "It's a prophet like the prophets of long ago." 16 Herod heard all this and said, "It's John, raised up—the one I beheaded."

Mark told us that Jesus chose twelve close disciples to proclaim the Good News and to heal (see 3:14–15). Now we see him send them off, each with a companion, just as he's had their company. Mark says they were to share his power to rid people of polluting spirits [v.7] and were to proclaim their trust in God by not worrying about their need for food, clothing, or places to stay [vv.8–10].

We also hear Jesus tell them not to worry about success, but to move on if their message is rejected, showing any town that refused to listen to them that they didn't take rejection personally—they could leave failure in the dust behind them [v.11]. So they proclaimed the Good News of repentance: you can embrace God's plans rather than your own [v.12]. When their message was accepted, it brought healing and freedom from oppressive spirits [v.13].

Mark says Herod heard reports about Jesus [14a] and also heard theories that tried to account for Jesus' popularity and power. He's not described as yearning for the Good News but, rather, as someone anxious to figure out how Jesus was attracting followers. In other words, he wanted the secret of his success [vv.14b–15]. According to Mark, Herod explained Jesus to himself this way: "He must be John the Baptist risen up again—though I'm sure I killed him" [v.16]. Mark makes the point that a collection of assumptions and some fanciful thinking are no substitutes for a willingness to learn.

A LOOK BACK AT WHY HEROD KILLED JOHN THE BAPTIST
[MK.6:17–29]

[17] Herod had ordered John arrested and locked away because of Herodias, who'd been married to Herod's brother, Philip, and was now married to him. [18] John had told Herod [probably citing the Pentateuch (Lev.18:16)], "You can't take your brother's wife as yours." [19] Herodias resented John and wanted to kill him, but she couldn't [20] because Herod was in awe of him. Realizing that he was righteous and holy, he protected him. Though he was baffled by him, he enjoyed listening to him. [21] But, as luck would have it, Herod held a feast on his birthday, to which

he invited court officials, military commanders, and the big names in Galilee.
²² Herodias brought in her daughter to dance. This pleased Herod and everyone
reclining at table. He said to the young girl, "Ask what you want. I'll give it." ²³ He
made her a solemn promise, "Whatever you ask, even if it's half my kingdom, I'll
give it to you." ²⁴ She went to ask her mother, "What should I ask for?" Her
mother said, "The head of John the Baptizer." ²⁵ She rushed back in and told the
king, "I want you to give me a platter with the head of John the Baptizer, right
now." ²⁶ The king was dismayed. He'd made the promise in front of everyone
reclining at table, so he didn't want to say no. ²⁷ He sent an executioner to bring
the head at once. The executioner left for the prison, beheaded John, and put the
head on a platter. ²⁸ He brought it in, gave it to the girl, and the girl gave it to her
mother. ²⁹ When word of this reached John's disciples, they went [to the prison]
and took the corpse away and placed it in a tomb.

———❧❧❧———

Mark says John the Baptist challenged Herod to behave as a true
leader of the Jews—that is, someone who follows God's commands.
But, according to Mark, Herod wasn't attracted to the idea that life
could be directed by God's laws [vv.17–18]. True, unlike Herodias,
who was enraged by John's words [v.19] and wished to kill him,
Herod was somehow fascinated by John's message. But though he
may have sensed that John's message was right, he wasn't quite
able to say how [v.20].

Readers may assume they know this story because it's been depicted in paintings, plays, operas, and films. But suppose the feast
was more of a symposium than an orgy [v.21]. And picture the
daughter as a little girl whose singsong gestures acted out a nursery
rhyme, not a seduction with veils [v.22]. Imagine the cooing of Herod's charmed guests, and the doting older man's outburst, "This
little princess deserves half a kingdom!" [v.23]. Then, all at once, a
delightful moment turns gruesome [vv.24–25]. How disheartening
to see Herod change quickly from a caring father figure to a craven
politician who feels forced to play the ruthless tyrant [v.26]. The rest
is silence [vv.28–29]. Then, a body is entombed [v.29].

JESUS' DISCIPLES RETURN; SO DO THE CROWDS [MK.6:30–34]

[30] Jesus' apostles returned [to Capernaum] from their mission and told him all they'd done and taught. [31] And he says, "Let's go into the countryside, just ourselves, to rest a bit." (So many people were coming and going, they hadn't a moment to eat.) [32] So, they set out in a boat to a deserted spot—just themselves. [33] But people saw them [in their boat], guessed where they were headed, and rushed out from every nearby town to get there first. [34] When Jesus saw a large crowd as he disembarked, he felt deeply moved for them. They were like sheep without a shepherd. So, he taught them many things.

—————

Mark describes the apostles trying to tell Jesus about their doings [v.30] while crowds [v.31] leave them little time for reflection. Mark has described crowds mobbing Jesus ever since the cure of a leper (see 1:45)—his house so crowded that petitioners came through the roof [2:2], people gathering in such numbers by the sea that a boat stood by for safety [3:9], and crowds keeping him from eating [3:20], forcing him into a boat [4:1], and besieging him upon his return from Gentile territory [5:21]. And once, the chaotic press of a crowd made it seem foolish for Jesus to ask, "Who touched me?" [5:31]. So we're not surprised to read that Jesus and his disciples felt the need to get away from the needy crowds [v.32]. But Mark says their plans for rest and reflection were foiled by yet more crowds—crowds whose need for Jesus' attention drove them to pursue him [v.33].

Mark says Jesus looked for a quiet shore but found a crowded beach. Yet he doesn't say Jesus was frustrated by not finding the quiet he wanted. On the contrary, he describes him as moved by what the crowd needed: care. His response to their need was to teach them [v.34].

Because Mark writes that Jesus taught "many things," we might wonder what exactly he taught—and how it addressed their needs. This is a trap. From Mark's first description of Jesus' proclamation of the Good News, Jesus' message has never varied: "God's kingdom is here. Turn to it. Trust in it" (see 1:15). Is there any reason to suspect that Mark is now keeping some new teaching from us? If we harbor such suspicions, we should read on.

THE CROWD IS HUNGRY; JESUS ASKS FOR A BLESSING
[MK.6:35–44]

35 As the hour grew late, Jesus' disciples told him, "This place is out of the way, and the hour is late. 36 Send the crowds away so they can go to the local farms and villages for food." 37 "Give them something to eat yourselves," was his reply. "We should go off," they asked, "buy bread that would cost more than a man can make in half a year, and then pass it out?" 38 "How many loaves have you got with you?" he asked. "Go look." They already knew. "Five," they said. "And two dried fish." 39 He told them to have the groups recline on the green grass. 40 Various groups settled down—fifty here, a hundred there. 41 He took the five loaves, and the two fish. He looked up to heaven and blessed the loaves. He broke the loaves and gave them to his disciples to serve the people. He also shared the two fish. 42 Everyone ate. Everyone was sated. 43 They picked up twelve baskets of bread fragments—and the uneaten fish as well. 44 The number of men in the groups who ate was five thousand.

———《❧》———

Here the disciples confront Jesus with three practical needs. First, it's time for dinner; second, people will have to go find food; third, Jesus needs to let them go find food [vv.35–36]. On the face of it, Jesus' response is ridiculous, and his disciples point this out to him [v.37]. Mark says that, when Jesus insisted they check their food provisions, they were sure of just how much they had—that is, not enough [v.38]. Nonetheless, we hear Jesus telling the disciples to settle everyone down for a meal—acting as though it was possible to be satisfied by what clearly looked insufficient [v.39]. So, says Mark, the crowd settled down for what common sense tells us will be a bad practical joke [v.40]. But at that moment, Mark describes Jesus doing what he's been teaching everyone else to do: turn to the Father in heaven [v.41]. And after he did this, everyone was fed [v.42]. In fact, according to Mark, there was a large amount left over [v.43]—even after five thousand had been fed [v.44].

Some have interpreted this scene as a miracle of generosity, not trust. They imagine everyone in the crowd digging into their pockets and coming up with more than enough to share—that is, taking care of their own needs. A report about generous human behavior is heartwarming good news, but it's not the Good News. Here, Mark doesn't describe Jesus asking people to find their inner goodness. He shows Jesus acting on his own teaching—turning to God for care.

ANOTHER LESSON IN TRUST [MK.6:45–52]

⁴⁵ *Jesus told his disciples to set off in the boat that had brought them to this out-of-the-way place. They were to head east to Bethsaida [where the Jordan flowed into the Lake of Galilee, near where John had baptized]. And he sent away the crowds.* ⁴⁶ *He told them, "Fare well." Then he went to a high place to pray.* ⁴⁷ *As evening fell, the boat was mid-lake and he was alone on land.* ⁴⁸ *He could see how they labored at the oars. The wind kept pushing them back. During the time of a soldier's fourth watch [somewhere between 3:00 and 6:00 a.m.], Jesus came to them, walking on the water. He seemed likely to walk past them.* ⁴⁹ *They saw him—walking on the lake. They thought it was a miasma, and they shrieked.* ⁵⁰ *All saw him. All were petrified. So he spoke up right away: "Take heart. I'm me. Don't fear."* ⁵¹ *He went over and got in the boat. The wind failed. They were beside themselves.* ⁵² *They'd learned nothing from the loaves. They had hard hearts.*

—⊷⊶⊷—

Mark has portrayed Jesus as a traveler (see 1:38–39). But Jesus now sets his disciples in motion [v.45] as he withdraws alone. Once before, he withdrew (see 1:13) to find comfort in prayer [v.46]. Though doing so now might seem to leave the disciples by themselves, it turns out that he hasn't left them alone. Indeed, he was acutely aware of them [v.47]. (Were they, in turn, thinking about him?)

Above, Mark described Jesus as touched to the heart by the directionless crowd (see 6:34). Here we see him touched by his disciples' plight, and going to them [v.48]. But what are we to make of Mark's description of Jesus walking along on water as if nothing was unusual—as if he might even pass the disciples by? We can certainly sympathize with their scream of disbelief [v.49]—a cry that suggests they hadn't learned much about God's abundant care, despite his feeding of thousands of hungry people. According to Mark, Jesus has to mother the disciples in their confusion, just as a patient parent would soothe a frightened child, saying, "I'm here; don't be afraid; think of God—think of 'I am,' the one who promised to care for Moses (see Ex.2:13–14)" [v.50]. He gets rid of the thing that frightens them as easily as a parent kisses away a scratch [v.51]. But the disciples aren't willing to be reassured by care and comfort. They've learned nothing from their previous experience of God's generous bounty. They cling to their fears; they resist the very comfort they seek [v.52].

MORE HEALING [MK.6:53–56]

[53] They made shore [after being blown across the lake], and anchored at Gennesaret, southwest of Capernaum. [54] As soon as they got out of the boat, people recognized Jesus. [55] News raced through the whole region. Wherever he was, they carried the sick to him on pallets. [56] No matter where he went—towns, cities, open fields, marketplaces—they put the ill in front of him and pleaded that he just let them touch the edge of his robe. Whoever touched became well.

—————

Here, the wind has carried Jesus and his disciples back to Galilee [v.53], where Jesus has already attracted much attention (see 1:39, 45; 3:7; 5:21; 6:34), and where he is now quickly recognized [v.54]. People spread news of his presence, and everyone who hears the news brings the sick to him [v.55]. Mark emphasizes people's response to Jesus' words and actions: they tracked him down and begged him to bring healing. And those who trusted in healing were made well [v.56].

Mark has often emphasized this last detail: the need for—and power of—trust. Jesus puts his trust solely in the care of his Father [1:13], and he apparently recognized that same trust in a paralyzed man and his friends [2:5]; he insisted that his closest relatives were those who did God's will—that is, turned to him [3:35]; his parable of the rich harvest taught that God's generosity can't flower without being accepted in trust [4:20]; he chastised the disciples for not trusting during a storm [4:40], but praised the lady with the blood flow for acting in trust [5:34]; and he was powerless to heal his old neighbors who refused to trust [6:5–6].

Over and over, Mark has depicted Jesus proclaiming in words and in works the healing presence of God. But we may wonder where the rest of the story is going. For instance, where do we imagine the disciples think their lessons with Jesus are headed? What might the Galileans be hoping for besides cures? In other words, what is there to learn from this teacher, Jesus, once one hears the Good News that turning to God brings healing? And what is one to make of the fact that, while some accept this news, others reject it?

SEVEN

Resistance from Jerusalem Officials; Acceptance among Strangers

SOME OFFICIALS CLAIM TO KNOW GOD'S WILL [MK.7:1–13]

¹ Some Pharisees and scribes had traveled to Galilee from Jerusalem. They mingled in the crowds gathered around Jesus. ² And they noticed his disciples breaking bread with unwashed hands. ³ You see, Pharisees—in fact, all Jews— eat only after they rinse their hands. This is a tradition from their elders. ⁴ Neither will they eat after being in public unless they wash. They keep many other such traditions; for instance, they wash cups, pitchers, kettles, and so on. ⁵ So the Pharisees and scribes asked him, "Why don't your disciples follow the tradition of our elders? Why do they eat with unclean hands?" ⁶ He said, "Isaiah captured you hypocrites perfectly when he wrote about you, 'This people mentions me with their lips, but their hearts are nowhere near me. ⁷ Their worship is worthless. They proclaim human teachings as commandments' [Is.29:13]. ⁸ You toss out the command of God and cling to human tradition. ⁹ Is it good," he asked, "to pull down God's command to put up your tradition? ¹⁰ Moses said, 'Honor your father and mother' [Ex.20:12a] and 'who curses father or mother must die' [Ex.21:17]. ¹¹ But you say someone can tell their father or mother, 'I've made all my earnings korban—that is, "dedicated to God."' ¹² You say that vow frees you

*from responsibility for a father or mother. ¹³ You void the word of God and pass
off tradition as a substitute. And you do this sort of thing often."*

⎯⎯⎯

Mark again portrays Jesus hounded by Pharisees and scribes (recall
2:6 and 2:24). Their first concern here is adherence to rules [v.2], for
Mark emphasizes their fixation on tradition, not sanitation [v.3].
These were individuals who were obsessed with conformity [v.4].

The evangelist depicts the authorities acting courteously [v.5],
but says Jesus called their politeness a mask [v.6a] and told them
what they already knew: Isaiah spoke against pious pretensions and
against imposing those pretensions on others [vv.6b–7]. Mark says
Jesus pointed out that they were putting their rules before God's
[v.8]. We hear him asking, "Does that make sense?" [v.9], and offering an example to describe how easy it is to pretend our desires are
God's desires [vv.10–12]—a pretense any child could see through.
We hear him conclude with some advice for these religious leaders:
if they reflected on their habits, they might find that they were
calling their wishes God's will more often than they thought [v.13].
They were ripe for the Good News of repentance.

JESUS DESCRIBES WHAT IT IS TO IGNORE GOD'S WILL
[MK.7:14–23]

*¹⁴ After his discussion with the Pharisees and scribes, Jesus called for the
attention of the crowd. "Listen, everyone," he said. "Understand this. ¹⁵ Nothing
outside gets in and degrades you. Degradation comes from inside you." [¹⁶ The
verse, "If you have ears, hear," doesn't appear in most ancient manuscripts.]
¹⁷ He left the crowd, entered a house, and the disciples asked about his short
saying. ¹⁸ "You don't understand either?" he said. "What goes in doesn't taint a
person. ¹⁹ Food doesn't go to the heart, but to the gut—then out. It passes
through. ²⁰ What comes from you is what makes you vile. ²¹ From the heart
springs evil thoughts of fornication, theft, murder, ²² adultery, greed, malice, lies,
lechery, envy, blasphemy, pride, pretentiousness—²³ all this is evil from within.
That's what makes you unclean."*

—=⦿⦿⦿=—

Jesus is described summarizing his lesson about God's will (see just above) by telling the crowd to notice what's inside them—what drives them [vv.14–15]. When Mark tells us the disciples asked about this summary statement [v.17], he notes Jesus' surprise [v.18a]. He depicts Jesus treating this lesson as so obvious that, at first, he merely restates it. Then he offers the image of eating to point out that our guts, without any special instructions from us, take care of what we take in [vv.18b–19]. Mark says Jesus noted that this process didn't touch the heart, or the heart's desires [v.19a].

He then describes Jesus giving his disciples an explanation of the heart's appalling capabilities. Destructive things burst out of us [v.20] because we brew them in our hearts [v.21a]. It's a menu of poisonous concoctions cooked up by selfishness [vv.21b–22]. In sum, it's our appetite for selfishness—our mania for putting ourselves first—that pollutes and poisons us [v.23].

This sounds like gruesome news, not good news. There seems to be little hope for us if our hearts are so vile—unless, of course, our hearts can be healed. And that's what Mark has said Jesus taught from the beginning of his ministry. Jesus has said: notice the state of your anxious hearts, and turn to the God who can heal them; be forgiven for your self-indulgent bumbling; receive kindness; rejoice in mercy. This is Good News—unless, of course, you like the mess you're in.

TRAVEL TO GENTILE TERRITORY, AND A HEALING
[MK.7:24–30]

[24] *Jesus left Galilee and went north to the environs of Tyre [on the Mediterranean]. He visited a house, hoping no one would know, but couldn't go unnoticed.* [25] *A woman heard about him; and because her daughter had an unclean spirit, she immediately went to him and threw herself at his feet.* [26] *The woman was a Greek—Syrophoenician by birth [i.e., not a Jew]. She kept begging him to cast the demon out of her daughter.* [27] *But he kept telling her, "Because children must*

be satisfied first, it's bad to throw their food to pups." [28] *"Lord," she said, "under the table, surely puppies eat children's crumbs."* [29] *"Because you say so," he said, "go home—the demon has left your daughter."* [30] *She left, went home, and found the child resting in bed—the demon gone.*

—⟨◦/◦/◦⟩—

Earlier, Mark said people came to Jesus from as far away as Tyre and Sidon (see 3:8), which is in Syrian territory, northwest of Galilee. Here, Jesus is depicted visiting a household in that territory [v.24]—perhaps to see a Greek Jew whom he'd met earlier. As has been reported before, news of Jesus' presence spread—in this case, to a non-Jewish woman whose daughter was somehow bedeviled. Like others who were desperate for Jesus' help, she pressed him with her need [v.25]. The fact that she wasn't a Jew was unimportant to her. She was only aware of her need [v.26].

Mark depicts Jesus driven by a different need. As he'd told his disciples earlier, he wanted to preach in all the towns in Galilee (see 1:38). In other words, his message was for his fellow Jews [v.27]. Although Mark told us Jesus once responded immediately to the voice of a demon bedeviling a Gentile (see 5:7), here he shows Jesus rebuffing a Gentile because of the narrow focus of his mission. But then he tells us the needy woman was able to change Jesus' mind, teaching him that it was as easy to give the Good News of God's healing presence to non-Jews as it was for children to give food to pets [v.28]. According to Mark, Jesus accepted her teaching—and, by doing so, demonstrated that he learned just as everyone else did: by attentive listening (see 4:23–25). Mark adds that Jesus told the woman that, because she spoke as she did—because she spoke from trust—her daughter was healed [v.29]. The evangelist notes that the woman found Jesus' promise of healing to be true [v.30].

MORE TRAVELING IN GENTILE TERRITORY, AND
ANOTHER HEALING [MK.7:31–37]

31 Jesus left Tyre, visited Sidon, traveled across the Lake, and entered the Decapolis [a region of ten Greek cities]. 32 They bring him a deaf mute, and beg him to put his hand on him. 33 Jesus took this man aside, put his fingers in the man's ears, spat, and touched the man's tongue. 34 He looked up to heaven. He sighed, saying, "Ephphatha"—that is, "Be opened." 35 Right away his ears were opened, and his tongue spoke—properly. 36 He insisted they tell no one, but the more he insisted, the more they talked about it. 37 They were utterly astonished. "What good things he does," they said. "He makes the deaf hear and the mute speak."

———◦◎◦———

Mark doesn't explain Jesus' trip through the Gentile region of Sidon [v.31a], or why he headed to the Decapolis [v.31b]—though we may imagine he hoped to see how the Gerasene man was enjoying his mission (see 4:19). What Mark does tell us is that, just as word of his visit to Tyre had spread (see 7:25), his arrival in the Decapolis quickly drew a crowd seeking his healing touch [v.32a].

Jesus is described moving away from the crowd to do what he'd been asked—to touch the man [v.32b]. But his touch is more than contact. He probes—perhaps to communicate his intentions. Though the man can't hear, he can see Jesus' moves; feel the push of his fingers; see him spit; feel Jesus' fingers on his tongue [v.33]. He could also see Jesus' appeal to heaven [v.34a]. In Mark's description, the first thing the man hears is Jesus' sigh of satisfaction—his exclamation of trust in the Father's healing power: "Open" [v.34]. All at once, says Mark, the man heard and spoke without any indication of impediment [v.35].

Jesus was described earlier demanding silence about his healings (see 1:44; 3:12; 4:43). Mark doesn't say why Jesus again demanded it [v.36], but he tells us what the people proclaimed when they ignored his injunction: their surprise. Their cries of astonishment suggest they couldn't quite believe their luck [v.37]. Their outbursts suggest how easy it is to muddy the Good News—which, though astonishing, is simple: turn to God, not yourself; be made well. When Jesus tells people not to speak, it's to keep them from mixing his simple message with expressions of incredulity.

EIGHT

More Compassion and Care; Unbelief; Suffering

ANOTHER HUNGRY CROWD [MK.8:1–10]

¹ During those days [visiting the Decapolis], a large crowd again gathered around Jesus. And they had nothing to eat. He called his disciples to him and said, ² "I feel sorry for this crowd. They've been with me three days with nothing to eat. ³ If I send them off hungry, they'll faint. Some have come a distance." ⁴ They asked, "Where can you get loaves for so many in this out-of-the-way place?" ⁵ He asked, "How many loaves do you have?" They said, "Seven." ⁶ He tells the crowd to recline on the ground. He takes the seven loaves, gives thanks, breaks them, and gives them to his disciples to offer. The disciples served the crowd. ⁷ They also had a few fish. Blessing these, he said, "Offer these as well." ⁸ They ate and were full. They collected seven baskets of leftovers. ⁹ Then he sent them off— about four thousand people. ¹⁰ He and the disciples then pushed off in a boat toward Dalmanutha.

Mark hasn't mentioned a move away from the Decapolis, so we can picture these events happening among Jews living in that Gentile territory. Here, crowds again gather around Jesus [v.1], presumably for the same reasons others have sought him: for his teaching and works. Mark, who already described Jesus being moved by people's needs (see, e.g., 1:41 and 6:34), again depicts him moved by a crowd's hunger [vv.2–3]. But we're told his disciples were overwhelmed by the obvious [v.4], just as they'd been stymied once before when confronted by a large hungry crowd (see 6:37).

So Jesus repeated this lesson: when they feel overwhelmed by needs, they should not trust their impulse to flee from those needs. They should do the opposite. Here, rather than preserve their meager rations, they should give their food away [v.5]—yes, all of it, even their few dried fish [v.7]. Then they could follow Jesus' example: give thanks to God [v.6a]—that is, trust in God's care.

As Mark reports it, the same God who provided manna in the wilderness (see Ex.16:4) cared for the hungry crowd—with plenty to spare [v.8]. The very large crowd could now be sent home content [v.9]. They'd been fed and, by their feeding, they'd been taught about God's care. Perhaps even the disciples learned a lesson. Next, it was time to travel back to Galilee [v.10].

JESUS CONFRONTS DISBELIEF [MK.8:11–21]

[11] [After Jesus returned to Galilee from the Decapolis,] Pharisees came out to argue with him, probing him and asking for a heavenly sign. [12] His spirit groaned in frustration, and he said, "Why does this generation ask for a sign? O yes, indeed, I say that if this generation gets a sign—" [13] He got back in the boat and went to another shore of the lake. [14] The disciples brought only one loaf of bread when they embarked. [15] So, later, when he warned them, "Keep your eyes open and avoid the Pharisees' yeast, the leaven of Herod," [16] they supposed this was about the lack of bread. [17] Realizing this, he says, "Why are you worrying about bread? Hasn't it dawned on you yet—don't you understand? Do you have hard hearts? [18] You have eyes, and don't see; ears, and don't hear. Don't you remember! [19] When I broke five loaves for five thousand, how many baskets of leftovers did you collect?" "Twelve," they answer. [20] "And when seven loaves served four thousand, how many baskets of leftovers did you collect?" "Seven," they say. [21] "Still no understanding?"

—⟨◊⟩⟩—

Here Mark describes a band of officials challenging Jesus with their doubts [v.11]. As we've seen before, Jesus can do nothing in the face of unbelief (see 6:5–6). Here, Jesus is upset that the Pharisees behave as children of the age, not children of God [v.12]. Because they were certain they knew the truth, they felt no need to listen and learn. Above, Mark said Jesus told his disciples to leave unwilling listeners alone (see 6:11). Here he shows Jesus following his own advice: he departs [v.13]. Perhaps because the departure was sudden, the disciples didn't have time to collect provisions [v.14].

Mark then shows Jesus turning the Pharisees' resistance to the Good News into a lesson. But, he says, when Jesus used the image of yeast to describe how a pinch of self-importance could poison a whole person—puffing up a Herod here, making Pharisees proud there [v.15]—the disciples had nothing but bread on their minds [v.16]. He says Jesus couldn't believe they were worried about provisions—that their hearts were still unmoved by all he'd taught them [v.17]. He describes him asking, "Don't you remember how I turned to God for help, and then there was abundance [v.18]; don't you remember that, although you bemoaned the lack of food, you managed to feed thousands, and to pick up leftovers—*twice* [vv.19–20]! Surely you now understand [v.21]." (Did they?)

JESUS ENCOUNTERS BELIEF [MK.8:22–30]

[22] *They land at Bethsaida. People bring a blind man, begging only for Jesus' touch.* [23] *Holding the man's hand, Jesus took him outside the village. He spat on his eyes. He placed his hands on his eyes. He asked, "See anything?"* [24] *The man looked around and said, "I see men like trees walking."* [25] *Jesus again placed his hands on his eyes. When the man opened his eyes again, his sight was restored—he could see quite clearly.* [26] *Jesus sent him to his home. "Don't go back through the village," he said.* [27] *Jesus and his disciples traveled north along the Jordan; then to Caesarea Philippi. On the way, he asked his disciples, "Who do people say I am?"* [28] *"John the Baptist," they answered. "But some say:*

Elijah; others: a prophet." ²⁹ "And who do you say I am?" Peter answers and says, "You're the Christ." ³⁰ Then he insisted none of them should talk about him.

———❦❦❦———

This scene depicting a trust-filled reception of Jesus at Bethsaida contrasts with the Pharisees' antagonistic greeting described in the previous scene. As Mark has mentioned before (see 5:28; 7:31), some people placed hope in Jesus' merest touch [v.22]. In the scene with the deaf mute (see 7:32), Mark said Jesus took him aside—as if to emphasize that he wasn't showing off for the crowd, but was teaching the man how to express belief in God's power to heal. Now Jesus again works privately [v.23a], helping a blind man entrust himself to the healing process [v.23b]. Mark describes the man as a good patient: he describes his situation as best he can [v.24], and he places himself, literally, in Jesus' hands [v.25]. Mark doesn't say why Jesus kept the man from spreading this news [v.26]. But Jesus' similar command after the healing in the Decapolis seemed aimed at preventing mere gossip about the Good News (see 7:36). Hearing the Good News accurately requires patient listening (see 8:21).

Next, we hear that, as they traveled north, Jesus taught his disciples the difference between spreading gossip and spreading Good News. First, he asks how others have been describing him [v.27]. After hearing the gossip [v.28], he asks what they've been saying [v.29a]. Mark says Peter answered the question succinctly for the group: "You're the Messiah" [v.29b]. But he doesn't tell us what Peter meant by using the term *Messiah*. He does tell us, however, that Jesus didn't want Peter and the others to include the proclamation of this title in the teaching he'd asked them to do (see 3:14–15; 6:12–13). It seems Jesus thought they didn't yet understand what it meant to be anointed and specially chosen by God. In the next scene, Mark depicts Jesus describing what it means.

THOSE CHOSEN BY GOD SUFFER AND DIE [MK.8:31–38]

31 [While in Caesarea Philippi,] Jesus began to teach his disciples how necessary it was that the Son of Man suffer; be rejected by the elders, the chief priests, and the scribes; be killed; and, after three days, rise. 32 He spoke this simply. But, Peter took him aside and admonished him.

33 So, Jesus turned back to all the disciples and admonished Peter: "Get behind me, Satan [the Tempter]. You're not thinking of God's ways, but man's." 34 Jesus asked the crowd to gather around with his disciples. He said, "You want to follow me? Turn away from yourself. Take your cross. Follow me. 35 You want to save your own life? You'll lose it. If you let go of your life, following me and the Good News, you'll save it. 36 What's the good of having the whole world, but not yourself? 37 What could someone give you in exchange for yourself? 38 If you turn away in shame from me, and from my words to this adulterous, selfish age, the Son of Man will turn away from you when he returns with all the holy angels in the Father's glory."

—————

Jesus is once again portrayed as referring to himself as the "Son of Man" (see 2:10, 28). Previously, he used the title to emphasize that, as a human, he is a child of God. Jesus seems pleased to call himself "Son of Man" because he delights in this relationship with God, even though the relationship will lead not only to his rising from the dead, but also to the suffering and death that would precede the rising [v.31]. Peter was not delighted by this prospect [v.32]. Mark doesn't say what Peter said privately to Jesus, but he portrays Jesus wanting to make his position clear to the disciples: "Yes, I'm tempted to seek a life without suffering. But to follow that human impulse is to abandon what makes us truly human: God's way" [v.33]. Then, says Mark, he explained this paradox to the whole crowd [v.34a].

We hear Jesus say that, if you're going to follow his example, you must be willing to accept the burden of living God's way. Yes, it's a burden, a cross, because it's not our way [v.34b]. If you want to embrace the life that God has shared with us, you won't cling to it

as if it were yours—because it's not; it's God's. Instead, you'll accept
Jesus' Good News that we can put ourselves—our life—completely
in God's hands [v.35]. If you do try to grab at life, all you'll get hold
of is this world's goods, because you can't capture and keep "yourself" [v.36]. Mark says Jesus asked, "Do you want to lose yourself
for stuff?" [v.37]. He describes him saying he'd chosen to delight in
the Father's way, and that all other ways were the way of selfishness. Then he asks the disciples to imagine what they'll want to
have chosen when he later appears to them in glory—when it becomes obvious that God's way is the only way to the fullness of life
[v.38].

NINE

More Travels — More Teaching about Faith

A VISION OF THE GLORY OF GOD'S KINGDOM — NOT
UNDERSTOOD [MK.9:1–13]

[1] *[Before he left the crowd (see 8:34),] Jesus said, "O yes, indeed, I say that some standing here won't taste death until they see the kingdom of God come in power." [2] Six days later, Jesus takes Peter, James, and John aside and leads them to a tall mountain where they're completely alone. There, in plain sight, he was transfigured. [3] His clothing became brilliantly white, brighter than white can be bleached. [4] Elijah and Moses appeared, talking with him. [5] Peter's reaction was to say, "Master, it's good we're here. We can make three tents—one for you, one for Moses, one for Elijah." [6] He didn't know what else to say—they were all stupefied. [7] Then a cloud covered them, and from the cloud a voice said: "This is my beloved Son. Listen to him." [8] All of a sudden, they looked around and saw no one—just Jesus and themselves. [9] As they came down the mountain, he told them not to tell anyone what they'd seen until the Son of Man rose from the dead. [10] Among themselves, they kept asking what "rise from the dead" meant. [11] [And they asked Jesus about a statement in Malachi that said, "Before the Day of the Lord, I will send Elijah to turn hearts" (Mal.3:23–24).] They asked, "Why do scribes say Elijah must come first?" [12] Jesus said, "Elijah calls for repentance. Then what happens? What's written about the Son of Man—about*

his need to suffer and be rejected? ¹³ *Suppose Elijah has already come. Suppose they treated him any way they wanted—just as it's written!" [see, e.g., 1 Kgs.19:14].*

——*☙*——

Mark doesn't explain Jesus' assurance that some of his listeners would see the power of the kingdom in their lifetime [v.1]. Is Jesus referring to God's power as it will be revealed in the resurrection (see 8:31)? It's not clear. What is clear is that Jesus wants his closest disciples to see divine power now—to give them a glimpse of his glory [v.2]. They see him radiating a splendor the world can't create [v.3] and talking familiarly with Elijah, the wonder-working prophet, and Moses, the first teacher of the Covenant [v.4]. Peter seems to think the vision should be captured and held—in tents [v.5]. In other words, neither he nor the others seem able to comprehend what they were seeing [v.6]. Mark says the Father concluded this encounter with a simple lesson. After wrapping them in a manifestation of his presence (see, e.g., Ex.40:34), he reminded them how to learn: "Listen" [v.7]. Then the lesson was over [v.8]. Jesus tells the disciples they would be ready to share this experience only after he'd been raised from the dead [v.9]. But Mark says they couldn't grasp what "rising from the dead" meant [v.10]—apparently because they thought Elijah must return and call again for repentance before all life would be renewed [v.11]. Jesus agrees that Elijah's call to repentance must be heard anew; but he asks, what happens when any prophet calls for repentance? Are they accepted or rejected? And what do his disciples think will happen to him because of his teaching about repentance [v.12]? Jesus also asks if they imagine that a new Elijah might already have called for repentance and been rejected [v.13]—nudging them to notice that John the Baptist died for proclaiming repentance.

JESUS TEACHES ABOUT REPENTANCE,
HEALING, AND TRUST [MK.9:14–29]

[14] When Jesus, Peter, and the others returned [from the mountain], they found the rest of the disciples surrounded by a crowd, and in dispute with some scribes. [15] The crowd was surprised at the sudden arrival, and they rushed to greet Jesus, [16] who asked, "What's this dispute about?" [17] A man in the crowd said, "Teacher, I brought my son to you because he has a spirit that makes him mute. [18] When it seizes him, it throws him down—mouth foaming, jaws clenched—and it curls him up. I told your disciples all this, but they couldn't cast it out." [19] "O, what a generation! You're without faith," said Jesus. "How long do I have to be with you? How long can I put up with you? Bring him to me." [20] They brought the bedeviled boy to Jesus. As soon as the bedeviling spirit saw Jesus, it seized the child, throwing him down, rolling him and making him foam at the mouth. [21] "How long has this been happening?" Jesus asked the father. He said, "since he was a child. [22] It throws him into fires, into water—to kill him. If you can do anything, take pity." [23] "If!" said Jesus. "All is possible for believers." [24] "I believe," he screamed. "Help my unbelief." [25] Jesus saw the crowd pushing closer, and he gave the unclean spirit an order. "Deaf and dumb spirit," he said, "I command you: Out of him! Never come back." [26] It bellowed. It gave the boy a terrible fit. And it came out, leaving the boy as if dead. Many even said, "He's dead." [27] But Jesus took his hand, gave him a boost, and the boy stood up. [28] When Jesus went inside with the disciples, they asked, "Why couldn't we cast it out?" [29] "This kind is cast out only with prayer," he said.

———◦◦◦———

Mark describes Jesus, Peter, James, and John rejoining the disciples who hadn't been with them on the mountain to witness Jesus' transfiguration. A crowd is waiting for them [v.14]. But, says Mark, the crowd's excited greetings [v.15] couldn't conceal the fact that they were in the midst of an argument [v.16]. We hear an anxious father get right to the point: "I'm relieved to see you because your disciples couldn't help me with my problem" [vv.17–18]. According to Mark, Jesus reacted with frustration to the failure of these disciples to learn his lessons about healing. Then, like a good teacher, he

begins to review his lesson—starting with the needs of the bedeviled boy [v.19]. It's reasonable to suspect that Mark emphasized the
grim details of the boy's suffering [vv.20–22a] to provoke our sym-
pathy for the father's desperate appeal [v.22b]. And yet we hear
Jesus challenge his appeal and question his trust [v.23]. But the man
responds candidly: "Of course I have trouble trusting! Help me!"
[v.24]. Mark's mention of the crowd's sudden crush suggests agitat-
ed curiosity, not belief. Jesus ignores this commotion, and simply
dismisses the spirit [v.25]. Mark says the crowd, misreading the
sudden quiet, pronounced the boy dead [v.26]. They were wrong;
the boy was healed [v.27]. Mark says Jesus dealt with the disciples'
puzzlement by spelling out what was implied in his previous lesson
in faith (see 8:20–21): one gives expression to faith through prayer
[vv.28–29]. Apparently the disciples hadn't thought to pray—to
turn to God—in their attempts to heal the boy.

TRUST IN GOD LEADS TO SERVICE TO OTHERS [MK.9:30–37]

[30] *[As they continued on their travels,] Jesus and the disciples passed into
Galilee—a route he didn't want anyone to hear about.* [31] *He was trying to teach
his disciples: "The Son of Man will be betrayed to men who will kill him. Three
days after being killed, he'll rise."* [32] *They didn't understand what he was telling
them, and they were afraid to ask.* [33] *When Jesus and his disciples got back
home to Capernaum, he asked them what they'd been talking about as they
walked along.* [34] *Nobody said anything. They'd been debating which of them was
the greatest.* [35] *He sits the twelve down together, and says, "You want to be first?
Then be last—be the servant of everybody else."* [36] *He brought a child before
them and held him there. He said,* [37] *"Whoever cares for a child like this, cares
for me—and not just me, but the one who sent me."*

———◦◦◦———

Mark has repeatedly described Jesus turning and asking for the
Father's authority, power, and care. And he's told us Jesus tried to
teach others to do the same: repent; turn; ask; accept God's care.
Now, says Mark, Jesus wanted to spend time alone with the disci-

ples to savor the truth he'd begun to reveal to Peter, James, and John (see 9:12): the truth that a violent rejection of him and the Good News would not be a triumph of unbelief and evil. We hear him ask them to imagine that this apparent disaster will actually reveal the power of divine life [vv.30–31]—but they're unable to [v.32]. Jesus' trip with his disciples (see 9:30–31) comes to an end [v.33a], but intensive teaching continues with a question about their conversation [v.33b]. The silence described by Mark suggests that the disciples knew their concerns about power were skewed [v.34]. When we hear Jesus tell them that greatness consists of service [v.35], we can assume the disciples already knew this. After all, they were all Jews whose lessons since childhood would have told them that God's greatness is revealed in his care for us. If God's greatness is his love and care for his children, how could his children's greatness consist of something different?

There may seem to be nothing great in caring for a child; even young, first-time parents can do that. But Mark says Jesus explained that the greatness of serving is in acting like God: sharing his instincts, loving what he loves, loving the life he created—loving him [vv.36–37].

NOTICE OTHERS' NEEDS, NOT YOURS [MK.9:38–50]

[38] *John spoke up: "Teacher, we saw someone cast out demons in your name. We stopped him because he wasn't one of us." [39] "Why stop him?" said Jesus. "No one doing marvels in my name will malign me. [40] Whoever is not against us is for us. [41] If someone simply gives you a cup of water in my name—yes, because you belong to the Christ—O yes, indeed, I say that person will be recognized and repaid." [42] [Again referring to the children in the crowd, Jesus said:] "Whoever toys with the belief of one of these little ones would be better off in a lake with a millstone around the neck. [43] If your hand hinders your faith, cut it off. Better to enter life mangled than to head off with those two hands to Gehenna [a place where roaring fires constantly burn useless sacrifices to false gods]. [[44] Some texts insert a copy of verse 48 here.] [45] If your foot is a hindrance to faith, cut it off. Better to limp into life as a cripple than wind up in Gehenna with two feet.*

[46 Some texts insert a second copy of verse 48 here.] 47 And if your eye is a hindrance, pull it out. Better to enter the kingdom of God one-eyed than go to with full sight into Gehenna, 48 where 'their worms keep eating them, and the fire never stops' [see Is.66:24]. 49 True, everyone will be prepared by fire—a salting by a fire that preserves. 50 Salt's good! But what good is it if it's not salty? Let yourself be salted; and be at peace."

———⟨∘⁄∘⟩———

John's question suggests he's puzzled by Jesus' command to love and serve—as if to say, "Certainly we shouldn't welcome our competitors with love and care!" [v.38]. Jesus' answer renews his challenge to the disciples' idea of greatness (see vv.34–37): if you share in God's work of freeing others from their demons—the very work Jesus asked the disciples to do (see 3:14–15)—aren't you sharing God's greatness? Jesus tells the disciples that healing doesn't reveal their power, but their faith in God's power. All signs of accepting the Good News—even the smallest acts of kindness—are cherished by the God who anointed Jesus to teach the Good News [v.41]. On the other hand, hindering the Good News is deadly. The awful image of being pulled under water by a great weight is a vivid warning against tripping up the young—and, by implication, other needy people—in their struggles to believe [v.42]. Mark offers three variations on another vivid image to emphasize how vital it is to avoid muddying the Good News [vv.43, 45, 47]. The Good News is an invitation to believe in the powerful presence of divine life: "Repent; accept the good news that the kingdom is at hand—that is, is fulfilled now" (see 1:15). When you accept the gift of divine life, you won't need the things of this life. You won't need your assumptions, prejudices, worries, or even your hands and feet! However, if you reject this gift, where can you turn? You'll have nothing but the empty pageantry of your pretensions; you'll have nothing; you'll have death. This lesson isn't new. The prophet who added the last chapters to the Book of Isaiah pointed out the same choice between life and death [v.48]—as did the author of the Book of Deuteronomy (see Dt.30:19).

Mark adds that Jesus said death's everlasting flame of regret wasn't much different from the fires in this life that purge and purify us—a purifying similar to salt's ability to keep food from rotting. Everyone undergoes this curing process; it's a natural part of life [v.49]. And the more you let the salting power of life work on you—the more you realize how little you know about life, and the more you let yourself wonder at it and learn about it—the more you'll see that the struggle of others to be cured of ignorance is just like yours. You'll begin to see yourself in them. You'll find yourself at peace with them [v.50].

TEN
===

Heading to Jerusalem, Teaching and Healing on the Way

JESUS IS STILL WILLING TO TEACH THE PHARISEES
[MK.10:1–9]

[Traveling south through Galilee, but avoiding Samaria,] Jesus and the disciples followed the east bank of the Jordan until they crossed into Judea, where crowds once again gathered. So, he taught them. ² Pharisees came up and questioned him: "Is a man ever allowed to divorce his wife?" ³ "What did Moses command?" he asked. ⁴ "Moses allowed a man to divorce by writing a decree of divorce," they said. ⁵ "Yes," said Jesus, "he wrote that provision because of your hardness of heart. ⁶ But, from the beginning of creation, 'God made them male and female' [Gen.1:27]. ⁷ 'So, a man leaves his father and mother and is joined to his wife. ⁸ The two become one flesh' [Gen.2:24]. They're no longer two; they're one. ⁹ What God joins as one, a man can't separate."

———◈◈◈———

Although the exact itinerary here doesn't seem important to Mark, we notice that the group was heading south—toward Jerusalem. Mark says that, when Jesus encountered a crowd, his response was the same that's been described from the beginning: he taught [v.1]. However, says Mark, some Pharisees weren't there to learn, but to challenge Jesus' right to teach [v.2]. Readers might feel the topic of divorce comes out of nowhere in this narrative. But Jesus' answer tells the Pharisees—and reminds us—that all activity is affected by the Covenant spelled out by Moses, the first teacher of the Law [v.3].

Mark tells us the Pharisees cited a rule about a husband's responsibility *after* a divorce as if the rule were primarily intended to allow divorce [v.4]. (The rule says that, if a man certifies he can't live with his wife, he can't later withdraw that certification in order to live with her again—see Dt.24:1ff.) We hear how Jesus deals with the rule: "That rule tries to set some bounds to selfishness; it doesn't give permission for more of it. It's saying, 'A marriage commitment doesn't allow you to keep your options open!'" [v.5]. Then we hear him speak of the relationship we have with God, our creator, who made us in his image and made a Covenant with us. The Pharisees, as a group of scripture scholars, would know the Book of Genesis and the words cited by Jesus [vv.6–8]—words that should have reminded them that the Covenant was an exchange of promises between God and his people. God promised to give the gift of life, and his people agreed to accept the gift of life—not undo it [v.9]. According to Mark, Jesus said the Pharisees had a choice: live in the world God made, or create a new one for themselves.

TWO LESSONS FOR THE DISCIPLES [MK.10:10–16]

¹⁰ When Jesus retired to a house with his disciples, they asked about his statements to the Pharisees [see above, 10:6–9]. ¹¹ He said, "Whoever divorces his wife and marries someone else commits adultery against her. ¹² And if she divorces her husband to marry another, she commits adultery." ¹³ All of a sudden, people brought children to receive his touch, and the disciples tried to keep them away. ¹⁴ When Jesus noticed, he became angry. "Let them come to me. Don't stop them. This is who the kingdom of God is for. ¹⁵ O yes, indeed, I tell you whoever doesn't welcome the kingdom of God as a child does will never be part of it." ¹⁶ He took the children into his arms. He blessed them. He placed his hands on them.

——◦◦◦——

When Mark describes the disciples asking for more information about what Jesus had just said to the Pharisees, he seems to suggest they didn't quite believe what they'd heard [v.10]. We then hear Jesus tell them what any child could understand: those who abandon one relationship for another ruin the original relationship—or, in fancier terms, adulterate it and break it up [vv.11–12]. (Children don't have to wait for marriage to learn the pain of being dropped by friends; and they know the cold comfort of claiming, "Well, I never liked them anyway.")

Speaking of children, Mark says a crowd of them arrived with adults who wanted them to experience Jesus' touch—an experience sought previously by others (see 3:10; 5:28; 6:53; 7:32; 8:22). The disciples are described trying to halt this onslaught (perhaps in an attempt to guard their privacy [v.13]) and, by so doing, upsetting Jesus. Didn't their most recent experience with the Pharisees teach them anything? People like those Pharisees—and, for that matter, like the disciples themselves—seemed to think that entering and enjoying God's kingdom was a riddle to be puzzled out, a test that had to be passed, or an honor that must be earned. No, we hear Jesus saying, it's for the asking [v.14]. Yes, it's for those who, like children, shout, "Pick me up!"—and who then expect to be picked up. According to Mark, Jesus says that, until we expect the kingdom to be given to us as naturally as a child expects affection, we'll never enter it [v.15].

According to Mark, for those who are not as finicky as the disciples—for people like Jesus and children—there's plenty of time to enjoy the giving and accepting of blessings [v.16].

A RICH MAN ASKS ABOUT SHARING GOD'S LIFE
[MK.10:17–22]

17 As Jesus continues [toward Jerusalem], a man runs up, kneels down, and asks, "Good teacher, what do I do to inherit eternal life?" 18 "Why do you call me good?" asked Jesus. "No one except God is good. 19 You know the precepts of the Law: 'Do not murder; do not commit adultery; don't steal; don't lie; don't cheat; honor your mother and father.'" [20] He says, "Teacher, I've observed all these from childhood." [21] Jesus gazed at him, loved him, and said, "One thing's missing. Go! Sell whatever you have. Give it to the poor. Make heaven your treasure. Then come, follow me!" [22] He frowned at these words, and left dejected. He had many possessions.

———≈≈≈———

In comparison to most of the other appeals to Jesus that Mark has narrated, this man's entreaty is surprising. His need isn't for well-being in this life, but for fulfillment in heaven [v.17]. Jesus' reaction is also surprising. He seems wary and dismissive — perhaps because the answer to the man's need is so obvious. The man should know that God, as the only true and good teacher, has already taught us the way to eternal life [v.18]. The precepts that spell out the life-giving relationship God wants with his people were set down in the Book of Exodus (Ex.20:12–16) and repeated in the Book of Deuteronomy (Dt.5:6–21). Mark says Jesus cited just some of them: to be united with God, one must never, in any way, treat others' lives as cheap; one must, in fact, give one's life to others; for instance, you must return attention, love, and honor to those who've loved you — your parents [v.19].

We're told that when the man's response indicated his question to Jesus was indeed serious — that he truly wanted to learn more about fulfilling his part of the Covenant [v.20] — Jesus' reaction was instinctive: he was moved by love, recognizing in this individual a fellow believer. So, says Mark, he gave him the invitation he gave his first disciples (see 1:17): give up the things to which you are now attached; give them to the poor who have nothing to attach themselves to; and follow me [v.21].

Mark tells us the man was unhappy with the decision he then made — but that he made it nonetheless. He turned away from the invitation to life that he had so eagerly sought [v.22].

THE DISCIPLES ASK ABOUT RICHES [MK.10:23–31]

²³ [As the rich man leaves,] Jesus looks on his disciples and says, "How hard it is for those who are rich to enter God's kingdom!" ²⁴ The disciples were confused by these words. So he says again, "You have no idea how hard it is to enter God's kingdom. ²⁵ It's easier for a camel to go through the eye of a needle than for a rich person to enter the kingdom of God." ²⁶ The disciples were completely baffled, asking one another, "Who's to be saved?" ²⁷ Jesus gives them another look and says, "It's impossible for men, but not for God. For God, everything is possible." ²⁸ Peter said, "Look, we left everything. We followed you." ²⁹ "O yes, indeed," said Jesus, "I say anyone who lets go of house, brothers, sisters, mother, father, children, or fields for me and the Good News, ³⁰ that person will, in this very age, get a hundred times more houses, brothers, sisters, mothers, children, and fields—along with persecutions. Then, in the time that's coming, they'll get life eternal. ³¹ Many of the 'first' will be last; the 'last' will be first."

—————

Here Mark describes Jesus offering a simple lesson: "That man, though he was obviously interested in learning what we teach, felt controlled by his money. Notice how the burden of wealth can narrow one's choices" [v.23]—how easy it is to be distracted from the kingdom [v.24]. Jesus is offering a lesson a child could easily grasp: there's no place in a needle's eye for a camel, and no place in heaven for riches [v.25].

From what Mark has told us about the disciples' lessons, we might imagine that, at this point, they'd be able to answer for themselves the question they ask about salvation [v.26]. We hear Jesus tell them that salvation is for those who need it. (You don't send an SOS if you can save yourself.) We can't create a kingdom of divine light and life; but, if we need one, we can ask for it [v.27].

Is Mark depicting a boast when he says Peter contrasted the disciples with the rich man by reminding Jesus they'd left everything to follow him? Did Peter think, perhaps, that through his generous efforts, he was building the kingdom [v.28]? Mark leaves no confusion about how one finds the kingdom when he describes

Jesus explaining the process. First, you renounce all other kingdoms (see Ex.20:3–6) to accept Jesus' Good News about God's kingdom [v.29]. You then discover the company and support of others who've made the same choice. You may also run into abuse from those who've made a different choice. But in that process, you'll find yourself beginning eternal life [v.30]. Our notion of building a kingdom and creating power, status, and prestige is, at best, backward [v.31].

SUFFERING AND GLORY [MK.10:32–45]

[32] They continued their journey up toward the heights of Jerusalem, Jesus always in the lead. Some people were excited to see him. His followers were afraid. He took the twelve aside again to explain what was going to happen to him. [33] "Look, I'm going up to Jerusalem. The Son of Man will be handed over to the chief priests and scribes. They'll condemn him to death and hand him over to the Gentiles. [34] They'll mock him; spit on him, beat him, and kill him. After three days, he'll rise." [35] James and John came up. These sons of Zebedee said, "Teacher, we'd like you to do something for us—any way you can." [36] "What do you want me to do?" he asked. [37] They said, "Make it possible for us to sit right and left of you in glory." [38] "You don't know what you're asking," he said. "Can you drink the cup I drink? Can you plunge into the baptism in which I'll be plunged?" [39] "Yes, we can," they said. He said, "You'll drink the cup I drink. You'll be baptized in the same baptism. [40] But sitting right and left of me isn't mine to give. It's for those already chosen." [41] The ten were angry with James and John when they heard. [42] Jesus called them together and said, "You know, among the Gentiles, those who are seen as higher up dominate the others. The hierarchy tyrannizes. [43] Not so with you. You want to become great? Become a servant. [44] You want to be uppermost? Be everyone's slave. [45] The Son of Man didn't come to be cared for, but to give care—his life for others."

—◦◦◦—

We can suppose the crowds were excited simply by Jesus' presence; and we can assume the disciples feared trouble from officials in Jerusalem (see 3:22; 7:1). Mark says Jesus confirmed the disciples' fear [v.32]—saying he'd be arrested and killed—but also said that, after the violent rejection of the Good News, the Good News would be seen to triumph [vv.33–34].

Mark doesn't emphasize the prescience of Jesus' words. Rather, he describes Jesus' acceptance of his vulnerability and contrasts it with the plans of two disciples for power [vv.35–37]. Jesus' response to his disciples' anxious hopes was to ask them if they knew how unsettling it was to give one's life into the hands of God—to be baptized into divine life. We hear him say that, like him, they will experience distress in yielding to God, but that they can't plan the outcome of their yielding. Someone else has already planned that for them [vv.39–40].

Mark describes how quickly rancor explodes when friends compete for the kingdom [v.41]—when they equate power with control [v.42]. He says Jesus told his disciples, if they wanted to follow him, they'd have to learn that God's power was his ability to serve [vv.43–44]. We hear them being assured that, if they were obsessed with the deadly desire for power—if their lives were eaten up by a need to dominate—they didn't have to remain in this deadly grip. They could accept Jesus' life—a life that allows the hand of God to direct and shape it [v.45].

AGAIN, FAITH BRINGS HEALING [MK.10:46–52]

[46] *[As they approached Jerusalem,] they visited Jericho. When Jesus left there, along with the disciples and a large crowd, the son of Timaeus, Bartimaeus, a blind beggar, was sitting by the road.* [47] *When he heard it was Jesus the Nazarene, he started to shout, "Jesus, son of David, have mercy on me."* [48] *People berated him for his behavior. But telling him to be quiet only made him shout louder, "Son of David, have mercy on me."* [49] *Jesus halted. He said, "Call him over." They called to him, saying, "You should feel grateful. Get up; he's calling."* [50] *He threw off his cloak, jumped up, and came over to Jesus.* [51] *"What do you want of me?" Jesus asked. "Master," he said, "let me see again."* [52] *"Go," said Jesus. "Your faith has restored you." He saw—immediately. He followed him down the road.*

As Jesus nears Jerusalem, Mark seems to speed up the narrative tempo: Jesus breezes through Jericho and draws a crowd along in his wake. Only a blind beggar sits still [v.46]—a beggar with confidence that Jesus will show him the compassion he expects from God's Anointed One—one in the line of David [v.47]. Mark says that when people objected to this cry for help, the man intensified it [v.48], boldly proclaiming both his need and his hope. This is in stark contrast to the hedging that characterized some responses to Jesus' power to help and heal. For instance, the household of the synagogue leader thought the appeal to Jesus was pointless [5:35]; the disciples were puzzled, twice, by Jesus' concern for a hungry crowd [6:37; 8:4]; and they objected to the blessing of children [10:13].

Mark says that only after Jesus responded to this boisterous cry of need did the crowd let the encounter unfold [v.49]. Bartimaeus was excited by the success of his appeal [v.50] and, when asked to state his need, he spoke frankly [v.51]. We then hear Jesus explain to him, and to all who are listening, that when you put your faith in divine care (see 1:15), you find salvation. Mark tells us Bartimaeus, confirmed in his faith, became a follower of Jesus [v.52].

In Mark's description of Bartimaeus' profession of faith, he could have used other titles. Instead of calling Jesus "Son of David," he might have said "Son of Abraham," "Son of Ruth," or "Son of Samuel." But David wasn't famous simply as someone whose trust in God had a powerful and comforting effect on other children of God. His name also became attached to the notion that someone in his line would be anointed to give this example of trust again. But his example would be more wonderful and powerful than that given by David.

ELEVEN

A Mixed Reception in Jerusalem

[1] Approaching Jerusalem, they arrive at Bethphage, near Bethany and the Mount of Olives. He sends off two disciples. [2] He says, "Go into this village. As soon as you enter it, you'll find a colt tied up. No one's ever ridden it. Untie it. Bring it here. [3] If people ask what you're doing, say, 'The Master needs it, and will send it back.'" [4] The two left, found the colt tied to a street-side door, and untied it. [5] Some bystanders asked, "Why are you untying that colt?" [6] They said what Jesus told them to say, and the bystanders let them proceed. [7] The two bring the colt to Jesus, put their cloaks on its back, then Jesus mounts. [8] Many others spread cloaks on the road. Still others brought tall grasses from the fields. [9] Those who led the way and those who followed cried out, "Hosanna [i.e., 'Lord, save us']. Blessed is the one who comes in the Lord's name [Ps.118:26]. [10] Blessed is the kingdom of our father, David—blessed is the coming kingdom. Hosanna in the highest [i.e., 'Lord, in the highest heaven, save us']." [11] He entered Jerusalem. He went into the Temple. He looked at everything. The hour was late, so he returned to Bethany with the twelve.

Mark describes the moment the disciples have dreaded—they've come to the city where there's official opposition to Jesus (see 10:32).

But Jesus is depicted acting without hesitation, provoking interest, even amazement, about his arrival. We hear him assuring his disciples that some people in Bethphage will respect him as a "Master" who wants to enter the city of Jerusalem on a colt [vv.1–3]—a choice that would remind devout readers of scripture of the image of a powerful but gracious king celebrating the great triumph of bringing peace to Jerusalem (see Zec.9:9). We read that two disciples found Jesus' assurances about the colt to be true [vv.4–6]. They then helped him prepare for his entry into Jerusalem [v.7].

Crowds are described showing great deference as Jesus rides to Jerusalem [v.8]. Mark doesn't say they recognized his mount as a sign of kingship, but he does say they loudly proclaimed their hopes: "Be our savior! Be like King David! Make us the powerful people we once were!" [vv.9–10]. Note that their cries were neither as simple nor as personal as the plea recently made by Bartimaeus: "Son of David, have mercy on me" (see 10:47).

Suddenly the parade is over. The abrupt switch from a noisy crowd to Jesus quietly regarding the Temple seems almost ominous. Mark says Jesus and his closest followers then simply returned to Bethany to spend the night [v.11]. What, if anything, had the disciples learned from Jesus' entrance into Jerusalem? There's sure to be a follow-up lesson.

JESUS EXPERIENCES TWO DISAPPOINTMENTS [MK.11:12–19]

[12] *When they left Bethany the next day, Jesus was hungry.* [13] *He saw a leafy fig tree, and went up to look for fruit. He found nothing but leaves. It wasn't fig season.* [14] *When he said to it, "May no one ever eat your fruit again," the disciples heard him.* [15] *They went into Jerusalem, entered the Temple, and he set about driving merchants and their customers out. He overturned the money changers' tables and the dove sellers' seats.* [16] *He wouldn't let anyone carry a chest, jug, or any other vessel through the Temple.* [17] *Then he began to teach. "Isn't it written: 'My house will be called a house of prayer for all people' [see Is.56:7]? You've made it a 'den of thieves' [see Jer.7:11]."* [18] *The chief priests and scribes heard this and wondered how they might get rid of him. They were*

alarmed by the fact that the crowd marveled at his teaching. [19] When it became late, Jesus and his disciples left the city again.

—————◦◦◦—————

Mark's description of an encounter with a fig tree might make us wonder what the disciples made of what's obviously another attempt by Jesus to teach them [vv.12–14]. He once used livestock in a lesson (see 5:13); here, he uses a tree. For the second part of this lesson, we'll have to wait for the scene described below (see 11:20ff.).

Mark depicts Jesus leaping into action as soon as he arrives at the Temple. The suddenness with which Jesus attacks the places of business [v.15] suggests he may have noticed this commercialization of the Temple during his visit the day before (see 11:11). We hear him insist the Temple has only one purpose and shouldn't be used for any other business—or even as a shortcut while going about one's daily business [v.16]. Mark says he drove home this point by making a stark contrast: "Remember what the author of the Book of Isaiah wrote; he told God's children to make this Temple a place where the whole world would turn to God in their need. Now, compare that vision with the reality you see in front of you: a pit in which you've decided to compete with one another for bargains" [v.17].

It's reported that, because the people were moved by this teaching, Jerusalem's official leaders felt so threatened they made plans to do away with Jesus [v.18]. This is the sort of reaction Mark told us Jesus described to his slow-learning disciples (see 8:31; 9:31; 10:33). But Mark tells us that, despite this danger, Jesus didn't stop going about the ordinary business of living [v.19].

JESUS EXPLAINS HOW FAITH, REPENTANCE, AND FORGIVENESS WORK [MK.11:20–26]

[20] *Early next morning, as they were heading back to Jerusalem, they saw the fig tree dried up right to its roots. [21] Peter, remembering, said, "Look, Master. The*

*fig tree you cursed has withered." ²² Jesus replied, "Put your faith in God. ²³ O
yes, indeed, I tell you if you tell this mountain [on which Jerusalem sits], 'Up! Into
the sea!' and don't doubt, but believe what you speak, it will be done for you. ²⁴ I
say: believe you've already received everything you pray for; so it will be. ²⁵ And
when you're standing there praying, forgive any grievance you have. Then your
Father in heaven will forgive all you've done against others." [²⁶ The line, "But if
you don't forgive, neither will the Father forgive you," strikes commentators as a
dubious addition.]*

Mark describes the group returning to the site of one of yesterday's
lessons (see above, v.13), and Peter's response to the dried-up tree
[vv.20–21]. We then hear Jesus explain what Peter couldn't work
out for himself: you can't be sure of achieving much by yourself;
therefore, put your trust in God [v.22]. For instance, if you truly
need a mountain to be moved into the sea, or if you need a tree to
dry up as part of a lesson, or, most importantly, if you want to be
raised from the dead, then you'll turn to the God who cares for all
you need. You'll ask him to take care of your need [v.23]. You don't
have to fuss and worry about your needs. In fact, you can let your
asking prayers be thanksgiving prayers, thanking God not just for
previous gifts but also for the fact that he'll keep taking care of
future needs [v.24].

Then Mark says Jesus spoke of forgiveness [v.25a]. The sudden
mention of forgiveness isn't a shift away from the subject of prayer.
Forgiveness is the purpose and content of prayer. For God is always
busy forgiving—forgiving our lack of trust and our impulse to care
for our needs as though we knew best how to answer them. So
Mark describes Jesus nudging his disciples to notice how they could
become impatient with others who see their personal desires as the
most important matters to be attended to. We hear Jesus say, "Notice how impulsively you try to take the work of creation out of
God's hands—how you assume things could be better cared for by
you; that is, how you sin. Do you expect to be forgiven for this sin if
you can't forgive others for committing the same sin?" [v.25].

JESUS CHALLENGES OFFICIALS TO RECOGNIZE THEIR IGNORANCE [MK.11:27–33]

²⁷ They continued into Jerusalem [after stopping at the fig tree]. When they were strolling in the Temple, the chief priests, scribes, and elders confronted him. ²⁸ They asked, "What authority do you have for your actions? Who gave you authority to do what you do?" ²⁹ "I'll ask you a question," said Jesus. "Answer it, then I'll explain my authority. ³⁰ Tell me, was John's baptism from heaven, or was it merely human?" ³¹ They discussed this. "If we say 'heavenly,' he'll ask why we didn't believe John. ³² If we say 'human,' well—" They were afraid of the crowd, for everyone thought John was a true prophet. ³³ So they answered, "We don't know." Jesus said, "Then I won't tell you what authority I have for my actions."

———❧———

Mark told us that, late on the previous afternoon, Jesus threw merchants out of the Temple and asked the people gathered there to remember the Temple's purpose (see 11:15–17). Here, his return to the Temple gives the authorities the opportunity to insist he defend his actions [vv.27–28]. Mark says Jesus' response was a request for a simple exchange [v.29]. Then we hear him ask whether or not they saw God at work in John's proclamation of repentance [v.30].

Mark says the authorities knew they'd rejected John's message [v.31] but were unwilling to say how they'd reached their dismissive judgment. And when Mark says they feared the crowds [v.32], he's telling us that these authorities wouldn't exercise the only authority they had: the authority to teach—the authority to join John in calling God's people to repent.

There's irony in the authorities' confession of ignorance [v.33a]. On the one hand, it's a lie; they do know the judgment they made about John's teaching. But they're also telling the truth; they don't understand how God expresses his authority through human beings. Mark seems to assume readers will know from other sources that the Baptist's message of repentance was challenged by some Jewish authorities (see, e.g., Jn.1:19). The nervousness of the authorities is similar to the anxiety of the disciples who complained when someone outside their group healed in Jesus' name (see 9:38) — their concern was for *their* power, not God's. As Mark tells it, the authorities hadn't learned the lesson taught by both John the Baptist and Jesus: children of God can act like divine children, trusting that God is the source of their power and the author of all the good they do. Mark doesn't explain how Jesus shared in God's power [v.33b], but presents him simply believing that he did share it. After all, now is the time of fulfillment; God's kingdom is here (see 1:15). The authorities, apparently, didn't believe this.

TWELVE

A Day of Teaching in the Temple

A LESSON ABOUT ACCEPTING GOD'S DESIRES [MK.12:1–12]

[1] [Turning away from the authorities,] Jesus offered the people in the Temple a parable: "A man planted a vineyard, surrounded it with a fence, put in a wine-press, and built a watchtower. He leased it to tenants, then traveled abroad. [2] In harvest season, he sent a slave to collect his profit from the harvest. [3] But they grabbed him, beat him, and sent him off without a thing. [4] He sent another slave. They smacked his head and taunted him. [5] The next one he sent they killed. The same with many others: beatings and killings. [6] There was one he hadn't sent: his beloved son. He sent him, finally—thinking, 'They'll respect my son.' [7] But the tenants said, 'This is the heir. Let's kill him and take the inheritance.' [8] They grabbed him, killed him, and threw him out of the vineyard. [9] What will the master of the vineyard do now? He'll come home, kill the tenants, then give the vineyard to others. [10] You read in scripture: 'The stone rejected by the builders becomes the cornerstone. [11] The Lord does this. We find it wonderful' [Ps.118:22–23]." [12] The authorities wanted to get hold of him, but they were afraid of the crowd. They knew the parable was addressed to them. They left his presence and went away.

—❧❧❧—

Mark describes the teacher telling a story: someone puts plenty of care into creating a vineyard and dealing with managers [v.1]. He then asks for his share in the deal [v.2]. The owner is remarkably patient with the rebellious tenant managers, who not only refuse to respect his rights but also think they can put themselves in his place. Such stupidity is hard to believe. Who could be so selfish—so blind to the needs, concerns, and rights of another [vv.3–8]?

We hear Jesus ask his audience, which included those who challenged him in the last scene [11:27–33], what they thought would happen to people whose selfishness allowed them to ignore everyone but themselves. Will they find eternal satisfaction by pretending they can grab all they want? If someone treated a binding covenant as though it didn't exist, what might happen next [v.9]? Mark says Jesus cited scripture to remind his audience, first, that self-assurance can close us off from fresh ideas, making us too ready to say: "O, that stone won't work" [v.10a]; and, second, that such arrogance can blind us to the fact that God can be at work where we least expect him [vv.10b–11]. Wouldn't it be wise, then, to let the Lord take the lead in your reflections, plans, and decisions?

According to Mark, the officious priests, scribes, and elders listening to this story recognized it as a portrait of themselves, and became angry [v.12]. But the parable wasn't written down in this Gospel for those officials. It's addressed to you and me. See any likeness?

A TRICK QUESTION FROM SOME RELUCTANT STUDENTS
[MK.12:13–17]

[13] *They [the authorities who turned away from Jesus' parable in the last scene] send some Pharisees and some supporters of Herod to [accomplish what they could not:] trap him with his own words.* [14] *They show up and say, "Teacher, we know you speak the truth. You never pander. You don't worry about public opinion. You go straight to the truth. You teach the way of God. Does the Law allow us to pay the tax imposed on Caesar's subjects, or not? Should we pay it, or withhold it?"* [15] *He saw their game. "Why are you testing me?" he asked.*

"Show me a Roman denarius coin." ¹⁶ *They offered one. "Whose image is this?"* *he asked, "and to whom do these inscribed titles belong?" "Caesar," they said.* ¹⁷ *"Give Caesar's things to Caesar," he said, "and God's things to God." They* *were stunned.*

———❦———

Several times before this encounter, Mark has depicted Jewish authorities as offended by what appears to them to be Jesus' disrespect for the Law (see 2:24; 3:6; 7:5). Here, Mark says the priests, scribes, and elders who dodged away from Jesus in the previous scene (see 12:12) have sent Pharisees and Herodians to make a second attempt at tripping Jesus up [v.13]. This fresh delegation of officials introduced their question—and set their snare—with perhaps a bit more flattery and unction than politeness required. We then hear them spring what they seem to have thought was a deadly trap: "Does the Law let you serve Caesar as well as God?" [v.14].

As described by Mark, these figures of authority played their game like would-be card sharks who can't keep a poker face. Nonetheless, we see Jesus playing their game. He asks to see one of Caesar's silver coins [v.15], then asks the obvious: "Is this, in fact, a coin of Caesar's making?" And they give the obvious answer: "Yes, it is." "Well, then," says Jesus, "it must therefore belong to Caesar."

According to Mark, Jesus then applied the same principle to God: the things someone makes belong to the maker, so you must return to God all that belongs to him. That would of course include yourself. What could these emissaries of the elders, scribes, and priests say to that? We hear they said nothing [v.17].

ANOTHER TRICK QUESTION [MK.12:18–27]

¹⁸ *Up next come some Sadducees [an association of Jews known for strictly interpreting the Law], claiming there was no resurrection. So they say:* ¹⁹ *"Teacher, Moses laid down the Law for us that, if a man's brother dies leaving a widow but no child, the surviving brother can marry her and raise children with her.* ²⁰ *Once, there were seven brothers. The first took a wife, died, and left no*

children. *²¹ The second took her, and died leaving no children; the same happened to the third, ²² and to the rest of the seven—death, but no children. Last to
die was the woman. ²³ After rising in the resurrection, whose wife will she be—
having been wife to all seven?" ²⁴ Jesus said, "Isn't this a misreading of scripture, and of God's power? ²⁵ When the dead rise, they don't give or take in
marriage. They're like heavenly angels. ²⁶ Haven't you read about the raising of
the dead in the Book of Moses—where God spoke at the bush saying, 'I am the
God of Abraham, the God of Isaac, the God of Jacob' [Ex.3:6]? ²⁷ He's not God of
the dead, but of the living. You're completely misinformed."*

—————

Mark brings onto the scene members of another semiofficial group
of community leaders. Their appearance right after a scene in which
Pharisees and Herodians tried to trip Jesus up (see 12:13) might lead
readers to suspect there's going to be another game of one-upman-
ship [v.18]. And such suspicions are right. Mark describes the Sadducees wasting no time introducing what they seem to consider an
airtight defense of their opinion: people would find themselves in
ridiculous situations if they rose from the dead after scrupulously
following the Mosaic Law [vv.19–23]. From their point of view,
therefore, one can believe either in the Law, or in resurrection from
the dead, but not both. Mark depicts Jesus as just as direct, pointing
out that these students of the Law seemed neither to have read
scripture properly nor to hold God's abilities in much awe [v.24].

According to Mark, Jesus suggested they might imagine eternity
not as a rerun of this life, but as a somewhat different, heavenly
existence. Such an exercise in imagination could shake up their assumptions concerning life after death [v.25]. We hear Jesus assum-
ing they'd read in the Book of Exodus that God identifies himself to
Moses as the God of Abraham, Isaac, and Jacob. This scripture pas-
sage pictures God inviting Moses into a vibrant, ongoing relationship that God already shares with Abraham and others [v.26]. Lest
the Sadducees—or we—misunderstand this point, Mark has Jesus
repeat it: if God is God of the living, all his children are living [v.27].

ANOTHER QUESTION, BUT NOT A TRICK [MK.12:28–34]

28 A scribe overheard this exchange, saw how well Jesus answered the Saddu-cees, and asked, "Which is the first of all the commandments?" 29 "The first," said Jesus, "is 'Hear, Israel! The Lord, our God, is the only Lord. 30 And you shall love the Lord, your God, with all your heart, all your soul, all your mind, all your strength' [Dt.6:4–5]. 31 This is the second: 'Love your neighbor as you love yourself' [Lev.19:18]. There are no greater commands." 32 The scribe said, "Well put, teacher. What you say is true. There is only one Lord; there is no other. 33 And loving him with all your heart, all your thoughts, all your strength—and to love one's neighbor as oneself—is greater than all burned offerings, all sacri-fices." 34 Jesus saw the man had given thought to his response. He said, "You're not far from God's kingdom." No one had the heart to ask more questions.

———❧———

Although Mark has described some scribes as suspicious of Jesus (see 11:27–28), here he introduces one who seems open to Jesus' teaching [v.28]. In response to such openness, according to Mark, Jesus taught by responding to the man's question. First, he iden-tified the most fundamental call or command that God gives to his people—the call to keep hearing the truth about the deal God has made with them. "Hear," in Hebrew, is *shema*, the first word of a collection of verses from the Books of Deuteronomy and Numbers that were repeated several times a day by believing Jews. Jesus says these verses (which state God's intention for his people) might be summed up this way: "Listen, I can take complete care of you. No one else can make this claim. So don't give your heart, your yearn-ings, your thoughts, your powers to anyone else." Mark says Jesus added: "Now, listen further. Because God cares for all his children, he wants each of us to see all others as he sees them—beloved. We are to care for one another as he cares for us" [vv.29–31].

The scribe is depicted as embracing what Jesus said. He didn't propose a different point of view, but agreed that nothing could be more important than these two relationships [vv.32–33]. Then we hear Jesus offer one last lesson, asking the scribe to notice that the relationship between God and his children, which both of them had just outlined, was like the kingdom proclaimed by Jesus (see 1:15) and promised in scripture (see, e.g., Ps.62, 69, 85, 97–99, 118). According to Mark, this conversation between Jesus and the scribe brought an end, for a moment, to challenges and questions (see 11:27–33; 12:13–17; 12:18–27). If we picture the crowd in the Temple suddenly silent, we might wonder how many of the people who shared the stillness were savoring the truth confessed by Jesus and the thoughtful scribe, and how many may have been merely waiting for another chance to air their doubts [v.34].

JESUS ASKS ABOUT THE MESSIAH, WARNS AGAINST PRIDE, AND PRAISES GENEROSITY [MK.12:35–44]

[35] Jesus continued to teach in the Temple that day. [For the day's beginning, see 11:27.] He asked, "How can the scribes claim 'the Christ' is the son of David? [36] David himself was inspired by the Holy Spirit to say: 'The Lord said to my lord, "Sit at my right as I put your enemies under your foot"' [Ps.110:1]. [37] David here calls God's chosen one—the Christ—'my Lord.' How, then, can the Christ be his son?" The crowd heard this with pleasure. [38] He also taught, "Beware the scribes who like to walk around in special robes; to be addressed by their titles in public; [39] who sit in reserved seats in synagogues; who take the places of honor at feasts; [40] who defraud widows of their livelihoods, and then make long prayers in public. They receive the worst judgment." [41] Later, sitting by a Temple collection box, he watched the crowd put money in. Many of the rich put in large amounts. [42] A poor widow put in two of the tiniest coins—scarcely a penny. [43] Jesus called the disciples around him. He said, "O yes, indeed, I tell you, this widow put in more than all the others contributing to the collection. [44] They gave from their surplus; she, from destitution—all she had; her whole upkeep."

—————ɷɷɷ—————

Mark says Jesus spoke of messianic hopes and asked his listeners if they agreed with scribes who said a descendant of David would be a Messiah—the "Anointed," the "Christ"—who would return Israel to its former glory, or if they hoped for something more. Mark depicts Jesus referring to David as if he wrote the Psalms, then asking his audience if they could imagine themselves hoping for the same thing the Holy Spirit inspired David to hope for. We hear Jesus say to his listeners: "David pictured God choosing a lord to reign at the divine right hand, and subduing all things to him. Wouldn't this lord be greater than David?" [vv.35–37].

Jesus then pushed the crowd to reflect further on what was important to them. Did they envy the way some of the scribes managed to wheedle their way into everyone's attention [vv.38–39]? If so, how did they think those scribes could afford to spend long hours showing off their piety? Who paid for such displays [v.40]?

Mark shifts the scene, with Jesus noticing how people gave financial support to the Temple, and calling his disciples together for a lesson in what it means to help the community worship God. Mark says he pointed out that the generosity and charity of the poor widow was greater than all the generous gestures exhibited by the rich. The lesson seems to be this: if you love God and one another (see 12:33), if you believe God has great things in store for you [v.36], and if you don't need to puff yourself up [v.38], then you might feel free—as the poor widow seemed to have felt—to give everything away [vv.41–44]. (Or the lesson may have been this: a poor widow is not able to give freely when her community presses everyone to be *seen* giving money. Indeed, obsession with such display could force the poor into bankruptcy.)

THIRTEEN

Jesus Speaks of Life as a Struggle

HUMAN ENDEAVORS TEND TO COLLAPSE [MK.13:1–8]

¹ As Jesus leaves the Temple [after a day of teaching (see 11:27–12:44)], a disciple says to him, "Teacher, look! What impressive stones; such marvelous buildings!" ² Jesus said, "See these grand buildings? Their immense stones will all be toppled." ³ Later, as he sat on the Mount of Olives overlooking the Temple, Peter, James, John, and Andrew went up to him privately to ask a question. ⁴ "Tell us when the things you spoke of will happen. What will be the sign of the end?" ⁵ Once more, he taught them. "Don't let anyone fool you," he said. ⁶ "Many will show up in my name saying, 'I am the one!' They'll deceive many. ⁷ But, even when you hear about strife or reports of warfare, don't be upset. This has to happen; but it's not the end. ⁸ Nations will turn on each other, kingdom against kingdom. There will be repeated earthquakes. There will be famines. These are but the first pangs of birth!"

———

Mark describes a disciple talking about the wonders of the Temple compound and asking Jesus to share his amazement [v.1]. But we hear Jesus invite the disciple to think instead about the Temple's eventual collapse and ruin [v.2]. Mark tells us that, later, the four closest disciples asked Jesus to tell them the timing of the Temple's

89

end [vv.3–4], but he doesn't explain why they did this privately. We can suppose they didn't want the others to know of their concern—or fear.

We hear Jesus answer them by saying many would vie for their attention and would even claim to speak in his name, but they should beware being deceived [vv.5–6]. This warning implies they'll want to hear what others tell them, but that they shouldn't pay any attention. Then we hear him tell them what they should attend to. They should notice that human beings keep expressing their destructive tendencies over and over again; that whole nations repeatedly battle with other nations and struggle for dominance; that the earth itself continues to create upheavals; that even the weather can undo our basic work of producing enough to eat. But Mark reports that Jesus said none of that should upset them. Instead, they should be full of expectations beyond their dreaming. Why? Because all these disruptive events are part of the beginnings of creation—the creative process in which life is still gestating and is not yet fully born [vv.7–8].

Mark doesn't describe the disciples' reaction to Jesus' encouragement to savor creation's unfolding struggle. The evangelist may have been more interested in passing on Jesus' description of the struggle to those who are reading this Good News.

THE DISCIPLES WILL FACE MUCH OPPOSITION [MK.13:9–13]

[9] *[Jesus was talking to his disciples after a day spent in Jerusalem.]* "Be aware," he said, "that people will turn you over to the local councils and thrash you in the synagogues. You'll have to stand for my sake before governors and kings, giving witness to them. [10] What's most important is that the Good News be proclaimed to all nations. [11] When they arrest and try you, don't worry what to say. Let yourself speak what's given to you at that moment. You're not speaking; the Holy Spirit is speaking. [12] Brother will hand over a brother to death; a father will hand over his child. Children will turn against parents and kill them. [13] You'll be hated by everyone because of my name. But the one who waits patiently to the end will find life."

———◊◊◊———

Just above, Mark described Jesus comforting four close disciples with the assurance that they were in the midst of a process that would give birth to something new, even though the process might seem like a succession of disasters (see 13:7–8). Now we hear Jesus tell them that, when they face cross-examination by councils of Jewish authorities, or abuse from synagogue members, or arrest by the Roman rulers, they should regard these moments of mistreatment as opportunities to speak of the Good News [v.9]. Their willingness to spread the Good News anywhere and everywhere is what's important [v.10], not their personal dignity. (Mark may have imagined these words addressed only to Peter, James, John, and Andrew. Whether or not we picture the other disciples listening in, we can be sure Mark wants his readers to listen.)

Mark then addresses the fear that modern researchers have found to be second only to the fear of death: speaking before an unsympathetic audience. He says Jesus told the disciples not to fret about their powers of persuasion or their ability to impress, for the Spirit would move them to tell the truth about God's word [v.11]. This is the act of trusting that Jesus has often told his disciples to try (see 6:50–52; 8:20–22; 9:19; 10:52; 11:22; 12:34).

According to Mark, Jesus then offered a short but grisly list of human horrors that would be some people's response to the Good News. But Jesus insists the final outcome of this process will be fullness of life. All one has to do is wait for it [vv.12–13]. This may not sound like Good News to anyone who's already set a goal and a timetable for fulfillment. Waiting for the divine design to be completed may seem less attractive than clinging to one's own plans. Nonetheless, here Jesus has asked his disciples to offer the Good News about God's plan to everyone. (That would include those who might not seem to be likely listeners.)

WHILE WAITING FOR FULFILLMENT OF GOD'S PLAN,
BEWARE OTHER SCHEMES [MK.13:14–23]

[14] [Jesus continued to speak to his disciples after their day in Jerusalem. He said,] "When you see 'the abomination of desolation' [see Dn.12:11] in the place it shouldn't be (take note of this, you readers), everyone in Judea should flee to the mountains. [15] If you're on the roof terrace, don't stop on the way down to take things from home. [16] If you're in the field, don't stop to pick up your cloak. [17] Alas for those who are pregnant or nursing then! [18] Hope it doesn't happen in winter. [19] There will trouble in those days such as has never been seen since God first began creation—and will never be seen again. [20] If the Lord didn't shorten those days, no one would be saved. But because of the Chosen—the ones he chose— he cuts the days short. [21] If someone says, 'Look, here's the Christ!' don't believe it. [22] False Christs and false prophets will be roused up. They'll give you signs and wonders to lure the Chosen Ones with lies. [23] I've told you all this so you may be alert."

———◦◦◦———

Mark here borrows from the Book of Daniel's description of how the eventual triumph of God will be preceded by violent attempts to put human pomp ahead of true worship—to replace the Covenant between us and God with adoration of mighty men (see Dn.9:27; 11:31; 12:11). Mark reports that Jesus advised everyone to flee fast and far from these exercises of raw power [v.14]. Fleeing in order to escape the deadly horror of false worship is so important that the image grows into an extended metaphor. This flight should be immediate and without a second thought [vv.15–16]. Many will need encouragement and help in making it [v.17]. (Mark could have extended this list to include the old, the sick, toddlers, and the lame.) The flight will be necessary even if there are travel complications, such as winter weather [v.18].

We hear the disciples being told that no previous painful experience can prepare them for the difficulty of struggling against the ensnarement of false worship [v.19]. How, then, can they survive? The Lord will make it possible! We hear Jesus remind them they are the Chosen; they won't be struggling alone to keep their relationship with God. They're in a partnership [v.20]. They should resist the distraction of other promises [v.21]. Other promises will come wrapped in marvelous packaging, but they'll be empty. Mark says Jesus told them to remember they were chosen to share the divine promise [v.22]. Indeed, all that Jesus has been saying seems aimed at helping them realize the need for constant watchfulness [v.23].

JESUS CONTINUES HIS LESSON ON WATCHING [MK.13:24–37]

[24] *"After the days of distress I've just spoken of, [look for what many prophets have described:] the sun will go dark, the moon will give no light.* [25] *The stars will fall from heaven, and all the powers of heaven will tremble.* [26] *Then you'll see the Son of Man coming among clouds in power and glory.* [27] *He'll send his angels to assemble his Chosen Ones from the four winds—from the extremes of earth and heaven.* [28] *Compare this to the fig tree. When its branches loosen their buds and produce leaves, you know summer's near.* [29] *So, when you see all this happening, know the end is near—right at the door.* [30] *O yes, indeed, I say this generation will not pass away until all this happens.* [31] *Heaven will pass away; earth will pass away. My words won't pass away.* [32] *No one but the Father knows the time for this—not the angels, not even the Son.* [33] *Pay attention. Stay awake. You don't know when it is.* [34] *It's like someone taking off on a trip, leaving the slaves in charge, and telling the gatekeeper to keep watch.* [35] *So, be watchful. You can't know when the Lord of the house will come; evening, midnight, or early morning* [36] *—or, perhaps, catching you asleep at his sudden arrival.* [37] *I'm saying this to you and everybody else: Keep watching."*

——❧❧❧——

Here Mark depicts Jesus summarizing what he's taught from the beginning: "Turn to your God, see him fulfilling the divine work." He says Jesus first reminded the disciples that various prophets had repeated certain images to prod the people of God to look beyond the here and now—beyond the world they think they know [vv.24–25] (see, e.g., Is.13:10, 34:4; Ez.32:7; Jl.2:10, 31, 3:15; Am.8:9; Hag.2:21). Mark also says Jesus used an image found in the Book of

Daniel: a theophany in which a human being arrives vested with divine power and glory (see Dn.7:13). This suggests that he, Jesus, is the Son of Man whose belief in the truth of this vision will allow it to be fulfilled [v.26]. Next comes an image that appears in the Book of Ezekiel (Ez.37:9): God will assemble his chosen ones from everywhere the wind blows [v.27].

Mark says Jesus gave the example of seasonal change in the fig tree to advise the disciples that, just as they expect warm weather after the fig tree comes into leaf, they should expect the end of this life—that is, the life filled with false prophets, wars, natural disasters, and personal failures of every kind (see 13:5–14)—only after they see such things as the sun going dark and the Son of Man arriving with divine power [vv.28–29].

When we hear that Jesus promised "this generation" would see these things, we shouldn't think Mark was reporting about the timing of events. After all, he's about to describe Jesus saying no one knows the timing (see v.32). "This generation," it seems to me, refers to all who live in this time when life is still giving birth—this time of labor pains (see 13:8). In other words, the Good News isn't the revelation of when we'll end life (as we know it) to take it up again (as God knows it). The Good News is that everyone will experience the life God has planned for us. Everyone who is experiencing "this generation"—this period of gestation before the final coming of the Lord in power—will see the plan of God unfold in all its glory [v.30]. Mark depicts Jesus saying, "Yes, the heavens you now see will one day disappear. But there's nothing to fear. This isn't the end of things; it's part of the beginning. Everything we see now will fade away. But all that I've taught you about turning to God—and accepting the gift of his kingdom—will remain eternally true" [v.31].

Mark says Jesus then told his disciples they wouldn't be able to figure out how or when all this would be accomplished [v.32]. They, and all of us, are like children on a first long trip, when cries of "Are we there yet?" seem quite reasonable to inexperienced travelers. On such a trip, a parent's explanations about distance, traffic, patience, and imminent joys only strengthen the children's conviction that no one understands how tedious the trip seems. We hear Jesus tell his disciples not to be like tired kids fussing in the back of the car: "Learn to watch. Keep an eye on the unfolding of God's plans around you" [v.33]. Then we hear an example of patient watching: if you were a servant in a prosperous household, wouldn't you be interested in your master's business? If he said, "I'm off on a trip. See you when I return," wouldn't it make sense to look forward to his return? You might even be filled with expectations about your returning master's report about the trip. Perhaps he'll say, "Remember that kingdom I told you I was going to prepare for you?" Of course, if you don't think the master is going to bring you such good news, you might not care about his business. In that case, you could just nod off [vv.34–35].

But we hear Jesus suggest that we shouldn't do that [v.36].

FOURTEEN

The Authorities Plot Jesus' Death — Jesus Plans to Accept Death

¹ Soon, two great feasts were to begin: Passover, and the Festival of Unleavened Bread. The chief priests and scribes were looking for an excuse to arrest and kill Jesus. ² "But not during the feast," they said. "We want to avoid a riot among the pilgrims." ³ Meanwhile, in Bethany, Jesus was reclining at table in the house of Simon the Leper. A woman entered with an alabaster vial of the purest, most costly oil from the spikenard plant. She cracked the vial open and poured oil on his head. ⁴ Some at table were deeply annoyed: "Why waste all that oil?" they said. ⁵ "It's worth more than a year's wages! That money could have been given to the poor!" ⁶ "Leave her alone," said Jesus. "Why heap scorn on her? She's treated me beautifully. ⁷ You always have the poor. You can always care for them. You don't always have me. ⁸ She did what she had to do. She anointed my body to prepare for my burial. ⁹ O yes, indeed, I tell you that wherever in the world the Good News is proclaimed, her action will be mentioned in her memory."

Mark shows us how wickedness can flourish even in an atmosphere of holiness. The Feast of Passover celebrated God's freeing of his people from slavery in Egypt, and the Feast of Unleavened Bread celebrated God's present blessings (e.g., the harvest) and past care (e.g., during the flight from Egypt). But, according to Mark, the very officials responsible for organizing these celebrations were plotting an unjust death [vv.1–2].

Recall that Jesus and the disciples are staying in Bethany (see 11:1, 12). There, while the authorities plotted, Jesus dined. Mark's mention that the dinner was at a house owned by a leper reminds us that Jesus enjoyed the companionship of anyone who sought his company. Similarly, the unnamed woman's extravagant expression of respect reminds us that Jesus has often elicited strong responses [v.3]. But Mark tells us Jesus' critics can't—or won't—see that there might be good reason for such surprising behavior. They were smugly confident, says Mark, that they would have sensibly converted the oil into funds for the poor [vv.4–5].

We hear that Jesus felt differently about this event. We hear him wonder why his dinner companions might not want to enjoy and cherish their time with him—why, unlike the woman, they take no delight in the message he brings as God's Anointed One. Mark seems to stress the irony of officials working toward Jesus' death while this woman celebrated life—a life that would abide even when Jesus' body was anointed in death. He says Jesus promised that such faith in the gift of life would be part of the Good News wherever it was proclaimed [vv.6–9].

A BETRAYAL IS PREPARED; PASSOVER IS PREPARED
[MK.14:10–17]

¹⁰ Judas Iscariot, one of the twelve [see 3:13–19], left the dinner [see 14:3] and went to the chief priests to propose a betrayal. ¹¹ They were delighted to hear his proposal, and promised to pay him. So, he started looking for a chance to hand Jesus over. ¹² The Festival of Unleavened Bread began with the sacrifice [of lambs to be eaten during the Passover feast]. That's when the disciples asked, "Where should we eat the Passover?" ¹³ So he sends two disciples: "Go into the city. You'll meet a man with a jar of water. Follow him. ¹⁴ At the house he enters, *tell the head of the house, 'The teacher is asking: "Where is the room I engaged for the Passover meal with my disciples?"' ¹⁵ He'll show you a large upper room set and ready. Prepare the meal for us there." ¹⁶ The two went to the city, found things as Jesus said, and prepared the meal. ¹⁷ When Passover evening came, he arrived with the twelve.*

—— ✺✺✺ ——

Mark describes Judas Iscariot — one of the closest of Jesus' disciples — as so disapproving of Jesus that he chose to side with the Jewish officials whose disapproval of Jesus matched his own [v.10]. Mark doesn't say precisely what drove Judas to his decision. But Mark's description of general indignation above (see 14:5), followed so immediately by Judas' action, is powerfully suggestive that Judas was seeking out people who shared his dislike of Jesus' behavior — people who'd been hoping to come up with a scheme of the sort Judas offered (see 14:1–2).

According to Mark, while Judas was working on the details of his betrayal, other disciples were worried about the details of the Passover feast. Perhaps Mark intends the situation to seem ironic: one disciple hopes to get rid of Jesus; the others don't know how to fend for themselves without him. As depicted, Jesus' remaining followers seem to have expected that Jesus had made plans to celebrate the feast [v.12]. Mark reports that Jesus had indeed made careful preparations — even with attention to such details as a contact who could lead two disciples to the home of the person whose services he'd employed in arranging the feast. The two disciples apparently also collected one of the lambs that had been sacrificed for pilgrims at the start of the festival [v.12a]. Then, says Mark, they prepared the rest of the meal around which the Feast of Passover was celebrated [vv.13–16]. Finally, the group gathered for the meal, just as Jesus had planned it [v.17].

JESUS AND THE DISCIPLES SHARE THE PASSOVER MEAL
[MK.14:18–31]

¹⁸ While they reclined and ate, Jesus said, "Indeed, O yes, I say one of you at table will betray me." ¹⁹ This threw them into consternation, and each one said, "It can't be me!" ²⁰ He said, "One of the twelve! One who shares my bowl to dunk his bread! ²¹ Yes, the Son of Man proceeds as it's written about him. But what a calamity for the betrayer of the Son of Man. Better for him not to have been born." ²² As they ate, he took bread, blessed it, broke it, and gave it to them. "Take. This is my body." ²³ He took a cup, gave thanks, gave it to them, and all drank. ²⁴ "This is my blood of the covenant, poured out for many. ²⁵ O yes, indeed, I tell you I won't drink the fruit of the vine until the day I drink it new in the kingdom of God." ²⁶ Then they sang psalms; after that, they left for the Mount of Olives. ²⁷ On the way, Jesus said, "You'll all flee in terror. It's written: 'I'll strike the shepherd, and the sheep will scatter' [Zec.13:7]. ²⁸ But after I'm raised, I'll go ahead of you to Galilee." ²⁹ Peter said, "Everyone else might flee. Not me." ³⁰ "O yes, indeed," said Jesus, "I tell you, this day, during the night, before the cock crows twice, you'll deny me three times." ³¹ "If I had to die for you," Peter insisted, "I'd never deny you!" They all said the same.

———=·ø/ø/ø·=———

Mark here depicts Jesus giving three lessons in repentance. First, it shouldn't surprise the disciples that one of Jesus' closest followers, one of the twelve, would turn on him. Jesus has repeatedly taught the need to repent—to notice one has turned away from God, then to turn back to him. He's also pointed out that scripture keeps telling us that struggles and apparent failures will precede God's final triumph (see 13:14, 19, 24–26). All human beings experience this struggle, including Jesus, the Son of Man. How foolish—how deadly—for anyone to try and stop this process by trying to stop the messenger [vv.18–21].

Second, Mark describes Jesus showing his disciples how to take him in rather than turn him away. He asks them to let his life flood into them as a perfection of the Covenant. If the disciples had asked how this complete identification with Jesus could be accomplished,

Jesus might have answered with words similar to those he'd used before (see 8:19–21)—asking them to recall the five thousand fed when he said the blessing (6:41) and the four thousand fed when he gave thanks (38:6). Here, in blessing the bread and giving thanks over the cup, Jesus is again seen doing what he'd often told the disciples to do. He asks the Father for what he wants. In this case, he wants communion with all his disciples. However, Jesus doesn't drink with them now. He's looking forward to doing so when his death brings them all to the full life of God's kingdom [vv.22–25].

The third lesson begins when Mark describes Jesus telling the disciples they'd all flee as one—citing the prophet Zechariah to remind them how the people's fear of God's abandonment led them to abandon God [vv.26–27]! Mark has told us Jesus taught repentance and reconciliation from the first moment of his proclamation of the Good News (see 1:15), and he here depicts Jesus telling the disciples they'd soon need to be reconciled with him. And he promises they'll find that reconciliation if they seek him in Galilee after his resurrection [v.28].

We hear that Peter couldn't imagine ever needing to be reconciled with Jesus because he felt certain he'd never turn away from him [v.29]. Mark says Jesus told Peter that not the passing of a single day—not even of several hours—would occur before Peter turned his back on him [v.30]. But we hear Peter tell Jesus he's wrong—that, even if he were tempted to turn away, he'd resist that temptation with his life. We hear that the other disciples were certain the same was true of them [v.31]. To us, the disciples may look foolish with this display of bravado. It highlights their lack of self-awareness. We laugh at the sort of bluster that ignores the truth—bold assertions such as, "No, thanks, I don't need directions. I'll find it!" What does our laughter reveal to us?

Note: Mark doesn't mention when Judas Iscariot went off to fulfill his bargain with the chief priests and scribes. But the lack of a break between the first and second lesson [v.22] and the change of locations mentioned after the psalm singing [v.26b] allow us to imagine him slipping away at this later moment. That would leave him at table for the sharing of the bread and the cup.

A second note: Mark described Jesus arriving at the Passover meal "with the twelve" (see 14:17). But, prior to that, he said "the disciples" asked where to prepare the meal (see 14:12). Mark tells us that Jesus exclaimed, "One of the twelve!" when asked who would betray him [v.20]; and, in the next scene, he'll describe Jesus telling "his disciples" to sit and pray (see 14:32). In other words, as Mark depicts the events that lead up to Jesus' arrest and execution, he hasn't been careful either to exclude or include disciples not numbered among the twelve. We can imagine them as part of these events—or not.

JESUS PRAYS AT GETHSEMANE [MK.14:32–42]

[32] They arrive at a place called Gethsemane ["the Oil Press"], and he tells his disciples, "Sit here while I pray." [33] He brings Peter, James, and John along, then feels overwhelmed with anguish. [34] He tells them, "My soul feels as though it were dying from grief. Stay with me. Keep awake." [35] He goes ahead, falls down, and prays that, if possible, the moment might pass. [36] "O, Abba, Father," he says, "all things are possible for you. Take this cup from me. But [give me] what you want, not what I want." [37] He goes over, finds them sleeping, and says to Peter, "Simon, sleeping? Not able to stay with me even for an hour? [38] Stay alert. Pray, 'Lead me not into temptation.' The spirit is keen, but flesh is weak." [39] He goes off again to pray, and prays the same words. [40] He returns and again finds them sleeping. Heavy-lidded, they couldn't respond. [41] The third time he returns, he says, "Go on sleeping. That's enough [of my pleading that you stay awake]. Now is the hour. Look; the Son of Man is handed over to sinners. [42] Get up. Let's go. Look, my betrayer approaches."

—————

Jesus and his disciples are once again described pausing at the Mount of Olives after leaving Jerusalem for the night (see 13:3). We can picture them stopping for a while on the way back to Bethany, or preparing to settle for the night in some enclosure around the Olive Press. Mark doesn't say what plans the group had for the rest of Passover or the Festival. He does tell us Jesus wanted to pray [v.32], and that he wanted Peter, James, and John to join him. His heart was in torment and he asked for their support [vv.33–34].

Jesus' prayer is expressed with the simple directness of a psalm: "Lord, I am deeply troubled; help me" (see, e.g., Ps.18, 31, 42, 43, 71, 130, 142, 143). His prayer expresses both the pain of helplessness and the relief of knowing where consolation is to be found [vv.35–36]. We can't know what Jesus was hoping to share with Peter and the others after he prayed, for he found them sleeping. On the walk to the Mount of Olives, Jesus told Peter he couldn't be faithful even for a whole day (see 14:30). Now it's clear he can't be faithful even for an hour [v.37]. We hear Jesus invite Peter to pray with the same candor he himself has been using with the Father: "Lead me away from the temptation to trust in myself" [v.38].

We see Jesus teaching them by example—he returns to his prayer and asks to be freed from his own desires in order to be filled instead with the Father's will [v.39]. When we see Jesus again asking the three to join him as he grapples with the temptation to choose his desires over God's, it seems as if the importance of this lesson couldn't penetrate their sleepy state [v.40]. By describing Jesus' failure to convince the disciples of the need for prayer in a time of distress, Mark seems to be aiming a lesson at us: "Notice how Jesus again and again allows himself to savor the basic act of reconciliation he's proclaimed from the first moment of his teaching." In this extended moment of torment and temptation, we hear Jesus repeating to himself the Good News he's told to others: "My God cares for me; he leads me away from my desperate desires, and guides me with his own desires." If similar words don't spring to our lips when we're in distress, we could borrow, as Jesus seems to borrow, from the Psalms. We could say, for example, "The Lord is my shepherd. I shall not want. He maketh me to lie down in green pastures. . . . He restoreth my soul" (Ps.23:1–3).

Then Mark concludes the lesson in prayer by describing Jesus demonstrating for his disciples what he meant when he'd told them earlier (see 13:9–13) not to fear the world's angry rejection of the Good News [v.41]: they could confront such fury head on. They needn't run away from it [v.42].

THE AUTHORITIES ARREST JESUS; HIS DISCIPLES FLEE
[MK.14:43–52]

⁴³ Just then, Judas, one of the twelve, arrives with an armed crowd. They carried swords and clubs, and had been sent by the chief priest, scribes, and elders. ⁴⁴ The betrayer had given them a signal: "The one I kiss is he. Arrest him and get him away quickly." ⁴⁵ He goes right up, says, "Rabbi," and kisses him. ⁴⁶ They grabbed him and arrested him. ⁴⁷ Someone standing by drew a sword, slashed at the high priest's slave, and sliced off his ear. ⁴⁸ "Do you come to take me," said Jesus, "as if you were arresting a thug—with swords and clubs? ⁴⁹ I was in your midst for days, teaching in the Temple, and you didn't arrest me. But let the scriptures be fulfilled." ⁵⁰ All his disciples left him and fled. ⁵¹ They caught one of his followers—a young man with only a linen sheet. ⁵² He dropped the sheet and fled, naked.

—⟨ɷɷɷ⟩—

Mark changes the mood from pathos to bathos. He tells us that Judas and the authorities planned an arrest that, with the help of weaponry, could be executed quickly and efficiently [vv.43–44]. He describes the plan unfolding quietly [vv.45–46] until it erupts in violence [v.47]. Mark doesn't make it clear who was responsible for using the sword. (Are we to assume the disciples carried swords? Did someone in the armed crowd thrust carelessly in a display of bluster?) Mark isn't concerned with the perpetrator of the deed but with the pointlessness of the action itself. He has depicted authorities who claim to be dedicated to law and order (see 2:24; 3:2; 7:5; 10:2; 11:28; 12:14), and told us that Jesus has called their behavior hypocritical (see 12:38–40). Here, with one bloody detail, Mark shows how sloppily justice was executed by forces belonging to the authorities. And he says Jesus asked this self-important crowd to notice the incongruity of their actions [vv.48–49a].

Then we see Jesus reminding his disciples what he said on their walk to Gethsemane: scripture reveals that a heart without trust will be overwhelmed by panic (see 14:27). The disciples are about to demonstrate scripture's truth [v.49b]. With one sword stroke, Mark makes the authorities' elaborate attempt to impose swift justice look inept. Then, with the loss of a sheet, he robs a fleeing disciple of all self-respect. We must suppose the man thought the indignity of running along the road without clothing was a small price to pay for his life—or that he wasn't thinking at all. He certainly wasn't thinking about Jesus [vv.50–52].

JESUS IN COURT [MK.14:53–65]

53 The arresting crowd took Jesus to the high priest, with whom all the chief priests, scribes and elders were gathered. 54 Peter, keeping his distance, followed him into the high priest's yard, where he joined the servants warming themselves by a fire. 55 The chief priests and others in the official gathering were looking for testimony that would condemn Jesus to death. But they came up with none. 56 Though many were willing to testify falsely, they kept contradicting one another. 57 Some testified falsely about his statements: 58 "We heard him say, 'I'll destroy this man-made temple and, three days later, build one not man-made.'" 59 But their testimonies didn't match. 60 The high priest stood up and asked, "Don't you have a reply to this testimony?" 61 He said nothing—no answer. The high priest asks, "Are you 'the Christ,' Son of the Blessed One?" 62 "I am," said Jesus. "And you will see the Son of Man 'sitting at the right hand of the Power'; yes, 'coming with the clouds of heaven.'" 63 The high priest ripped his tunic. "Do we need more testimony?" he asked. 64 "You heard the blasphemy. What's your decision?" They all pronounced the verdict of death. 65 Some then spat at him. Some covered his eyes and hit him, saying, "Prophesy!" The servants greeted him by smacking him.

—————

Mark doesn't tell us what Peter hoped to accomplish by safely trailing Jesus as he was hauled before an assembly of Jewish officials. All we hear is that he managed to keep himself warm [vv.53–54]. Meanwhile, Mark's description of the trial emphasizes that the authorities' search for a capital crime was a sloppily played, poorly rehearsed charade with which Jesus was asked to cooperate [vv.55–60].

The authorities described by Mark seem uncertain how to make their case. But Jesus is portrayed as sure of the truth about himself. We see him displaying the confidence he asked his disciples to have (see 13:9–10), and describing himself being enthroned by God at his right hand and being sent by God to bring the glory of the kingdom to the world [vv.61–62] — the same Good News he proclaimed to his disciples in previous scenes (see 12:35–36; 13:26). Mark has never told us what the disciples thought about Jesus' description of his future glory, but here he says the high priest and his fellow conspirators were horrified by it. As far as they were concerned, to speak of sharing God's glory as Jesus did was to speak against God — to blaspheme; to pervert the divine truth [vv.63–64]. In this section of his narrative, Mark describes an assembly of religious authorities reviling not only Jesus but also the Good News he had proclaimed for them — and doing so with such angry abandon that their servants couldn't resist joining in [v.65].

PETER DISCOVERS HIS FAITHLESSNESS [MK.14:66–72]

"As Peter waits in the yard, one of the high priest's maids comes by. ⁶⁷ Seeing Peter warming himself, she says, "You're with the Nazarene, Jesus." ⁶⁸ He denied it: "I don't see . . . I don't understand what you're saying." Then he moved to the gate. A cock crowed. ⁶⁹ The maid saw him later and said to others nearby, "This is one of them." ⁷⁰ He denied it again. But then some of the bystanders said, "You must be one of them—you're a Galilean." ⁷¹ He started to curse. Then he swore, "I don't know this man you're talking about." ⁷² Just then a second cock crowed. Peter remembered Jesus' words to him: "Before the cock crows twice, you'll deny me three times." He was undone, and he wept.

—⎯⎯◦◦◦⎯⎯—

Mark describes Peter's response to questions about his relationship with Jesus as the opposite of Jesus' reaction to his accusers. When asked about his connection to "the Nazarene," he not only says nothing about the Good News that Jesus clearly asked him and the other apostles to share with the whole world (see 3:14; 6:7;

13:10–11), but also feigned ignorance about the woman's comments [vv.66–68]. Throughout this Gospel, from his earliest ministry (see 1:38) to his latest confrontation with opponents (see 14:62), Jesus has been depicted as ready to teach the truth of the Good News to anyone who would listen to him. But we hear Peter reply to one maid's curiosity with self-protective bluster. He doesn't seem to trust Jesus' promise that the Spirit would help him respond to anyone who sought to learn something about Jesus (see 13:11).

According to Mark, the maid's first expression of curiosity grew into something closer to certainty about Peter's identity: "This must be a follower" [v.69]. Then Peter's second denial provokes rather than lessens interest in him [v.70]. We can suppose his cursing had the effect that violent verbal outbursts often have on casual onlookers—stunning the bystanders into attentive silence. Is so, we hear that Peter took advantage of the silence to swear an oath to them—perhaps even calling God to witness the truth about him. Then he lied [v.71].

Mark says a second cock crowed, and Peter recalled Jesus' words to him (see 14:30). Peter is described as being shocked into realizing a truth he'd been successfully hiding behind a pose of noisy self-assurance. In Mark's depiction of him, he learns he's not a person of faith or someone who could be trusted; he learns that, like everyone else, he is a sinner [v.72].

FIFTEEN

Death Sentence, Execution, Burial

THE ROMAN GOVERNOR IS ASKED TO PASS SENTENCE
[MK.15:1–15]

[1] Early in the morning, the chief priests, scribes, elders, and the Sanhedrin—the Jewish high council—agreed on a decision: move Jesus, under arrest, to the custody of Pilate. [2] Pilate asked him, "Are you King of the Jews?" "These are your words," says Jesus. [3] The chief priests were accusing him of many things; [4] so Pilate says, "Have you nothing to say to all their accusations?" [5] Jesus said nothing further to him. This surprised Pilate. [6] Now, at Passover, Pilate would free one prisoner requested by the people. [7] Barabbas was a convict condemned for a murder during a riot. [8] So, when a crowd gathered, asking about the expected pardon and release, [9] Pilate says, "Do you want me to release the King of the Jews?" [10] (He could see that the chief priests had handed Jesus over to him out of envy.) [11] But the chief priests got the crowd to demand the release of Barabbas. [12] "What should I do with the King of the Jews?" he asked. [13] They yelled back, "Crucify him." [14] "What's his crime?" said Pilate. But they yelled louder, "Crucify him." [15] Wanting to appease the crowd, Pilate freed Barabbas. He ordered his guard to flog Jesus and crucify him.

Mark says the Jerusalem authorities presented their case to Pilate [v.1] by letting him assume Jesus claimed to be a king (a threat to Roman authority) rather than the "Christ" (see 14:61–62). As Mark describes him, Pilate knows nothing of Jesus' proclamation that, if we turn away from our fixation on earthly power, we can accept God's gift of divine power. He's interested only in solving a political problem—about which Jesus says nothing [v.2]. Mark has told us the case against Jesus was a mess of contradictions (see 14:59). Here, Jesus' indifference to the machinations of the authorities seems to puzzle Pilate. But it doesn't pique his curiosity [vv.3–5]. He's like the people of Nazareth (see 6:5–6) who couldn't imagine anything but intricacies of human ambition and power.

We hear that, with the gathering of a crowd to petition for the traditional release of a convict, Pilate thought he saw a way to get rid of this flimsy case without accusing the chief priests and others of bad faith [vv.6, 8–10]. But Mark reports that the chief priests parried Pilate's move with one of their own, and that the crowd boisterously demanded a death rather than give any thought to the question of kingship [vv.11–13]. As Mark depicts him, Pilate retained some interest in justice [v.14a], but quickly abandoned it when the cost of justice might be a riot at a time when the city was filled with Passover pilgrims. Mark says Pilate made the politic move of giving the crowd what they said they wanted [vv.14b–15].

EXECUTION [MK.15:16–32]

[16] *Pilate's guard took the prisoner to the inner courtyard of the Praetorium—the governor's official headquarters. There, they call up all the soldiers on duty.* [17] *They drape him in purple and put a crown of thorns on his head.* [18] *They salute him: "Hail, King of the Jews."* [19] *They smack him on the head with a stick, spit on him, and bend their knees to him.* [20] *When they finished their game, they took off the purple drape, put him back into his own clothes, and took him away to crucify him.* [21] *Simon of Cyrene, father of Alexander and Rufus, happens to be coming into the city from the countryside. They make him carry his cross.* [22] *They bring him to Golgotha—the "Skull-Shaped Place."* [23] *They offer him myrrh-*

sweetened wine, but he doesn't take it. ²⁴ They put him on the cross. They split up his garments by gambling for them. ²⁵ It was the third hour of the day [9:00 a.m.] when they put him on the cross. ²⁶ A placard describing his offense hung above him: "King of the Jews." ²⁷ They crucified two criminals on either side of him. [²⁸ A line here, "Scripture spoke truly, saying: 'he joined the wicked,'" is considered a late addition.] ²⁹ Passersby mocked him. Wagging their heads, they said, "Ha! He could demolish the Temple and repair it in three days! ³⁰ Repair yourself! Come down from the cross!" ³¹ The chief priests joked with the scribes, "He saved others. He can't save himself. ³² As the 'Christ,' the 'King of Israel,' he should come down from the cross. Then we'll see! Then we'll believe!" The criminals crucified with him also jeered at him.

—·—

Mark depicts a scene of gruesome farce as the soldiers have fun toying with a condemned man who is under their complete control [vv.16–20]. As representatives of Roman authority, they even have the power to force a passing stranger to assist them [v.21]. By naming the stranger, and telling us about his family, Mark reminds us that a legally ruling authority is carrying out an execution that involves actual people. This is not a parable about human power; this is a factual description of some of its workings.

Mark describes Jesus being taken to a specific place set aside for executions [v.22], and depicts how the execution followed a particular routine: the condemned was offered a sedative [v.23]; after he was hoisted in place, his effects were disposed of [v.24]; the operation was kept on schedule [v.25]; the offense was officially announced [v.26]; and these tasks were repeated with other criminals [v.27]. When the practical business was concluded, the farce could resume. The details Mark gives us about Jesus' execution seem to make a mockery of all his lessons about trusting in God. According to Mark, even the other condemned men found such Good News laughable [vv.29–32].

DEATH AND BURIAL [MK.15:33–47]

³³ At noon, darkness fell everywhere until three. ³⁴ Then Jesus prayed loudly, "Eloi, Eloi, lema sabachthani"—that is, "My God, my God, why have you left me?" [Ps.22]. ³⁵ When bystanders heard this, they said, "Listen, he's calling for Elijah." ³⁶ Someone soaked a sponge in the [guards'] thirst-quenching punch and put it up to his mouth on a pole. "Let's see if Elijah comes to take him down!" ³⁷ Jesus let out a loud sound that was his last breath. ³⁸ The Temple curtain was ripped in two—top to bottom. ³⁹ Standing in front of Jesus was the centurion in charge. When he saw him gasp, he said, "Truly this man was the Son of God." ⁴⁰ Standing farther away, women were watching. There was Mary Magdalene, Mary the mother of James-the-younger and Joses, and Salome ⁴¹ —women who'd followed him in Galilee and helped him—plus many other women who'd come up to Jerusalem with him. ⁴² Evening came on—the last opportunity to prepare for the Sabbath. ⁴³ So Joseph of Arimathea, an important Jewish council member who sought the kingdom of God, dared to go to Pilate and ask for the body. ⁴⁴ Pilate, surprised he was dead, called the centurion and asked if he'd already died. ⁴⁵ So informed by the centurion, he let Joseph have the corpse. ⁴⁶ After buying linen cloth and taking him down, Joseph wrapped him in the cloth and put him in a tomb cut out of the rock. He rolled a stone in front of the tomb's entrance. ⁴⁷ Mary Magdalene and Mary the mother of Joses watched where he was placed.

—◦◦◦—

Mark describes contradictory responses to the approach of death. After a prolonged gloom, Jesus began to pray Psalm 22—a prayer asking for help in a moment of deep distress. But we hear that neither Jesus' prayer nor the peculiar darkness kept a bystander from turning the confusion over Jesus' words into a joke: "Did he say, 'Elijah'? Give him a drink so he doesn't pass out before Elijah comes to save him!" (see Mal.3:23). He scoffs not only at Jesus' condition, but also at the idea that anyone could save him from it [vv.33–36].

Once Jesus dies [v.37], Mark instantly shifts the mood away from any hint of jeering or joking by describing the tearing of the Temple curtain [v.38]. That detail provokes an obvious question: What's going on? Mark answers the question by describing three reactions to Jesus' dying. A Gentile executioner proclaims the presence of God [v.39]; women disciples remain with Jesus, though he's dead [vv.40–41]; a member of the Jewish council, without regard for himself, treats Jesus' corpse with respect and care [vv.42–46]. Mark has shown us witnesses of this execution who enjoyed the spectacle of what looked like defeat, death, destruction. But Mark also depicts witnesses who behave as though more than death is at work. Could God be at work in this event, and could anyone hope the promise of the kingdom might be fulfilled through it? When Mark tells us that the women continued to be attentive, to watch, and to wait, is he describing more than mourning [v.47]?

SIXTEEN

Rising from the Dead—Spreading the Good News

WOMEN DISCIPLES FIND THE TOMB EMPTY, THEN FAIL
TO FULFILL A MISSION [MK.16:1–8]

¹ After the Sabbath [on the morning of the third day of Jesus' rest in the tomb], Mary Magdalene, Mary the mother of James, and Salome brought spices to anoint the body. ² Very early that first day of that week, as the sun was rising, they approach the tomb, ³ saying, "Who's going to roll the stone back for us?" ⁴ Looking ahead, they see the very large stone rolled away. ⁵ Entering the tomb, they saw a young man sitting off to the right, dressed in white robes. They were dismayed. ⁶ "Don't be upset," he said. "You're looking for Jesus, the Nazarene, the one crucified. He's raised. He's not here. See where they placed him? ⁷ Now, go tell his disciples and Peter, 'He's going ahead of you to Galilee. You'll see him there, just as he told you'" [see 14:28]. ⁸ After leaving the tomb, they fled. They were shaking from shock, and told no one anything, they were so afraid.

———ぴ∽ぴ———

Mark depicts the women who had remained with Jesus after his death now returning after observing the Sabbath rest to do the anointing [v.1] they hadn't had time to accomplish earlier (see 15:42). Mark reports their worry about the practical problem of entering the firmly closed tomb, but then says their worry turned to horror when it seemed that someone had not only entered the tomb but also removed the body [vv.2–5].

As Mark tells it, the young man they saw in the tomb had information for them, and a mission. He told them the truth about Jesus' resurrection—which, as disciples, the women had already been taught (see 8:31b; 9:31b; 10:34b)—and he told them to get Peter to assemble all the disciples in Galilee [vv.6–7], where Jesus had promised to meet them (see 14:28). Mark says the women were dumbfounded and did not carry out their mission [v.8]. Despite Jesus' lessons to them, they apparently didn't ask themselves, "What if it's true?" They didn't yet believe the Good News.

Many ancient copies of the Gospel according to Mark conclude at this point. A narration that started with the words, "This is the beginning of the Good News of Jesus, the Christ," ends with fear and silence. Of course, we who are reading this news now needn't be silent. We could accept the mission the messenger in the tomb gave the women. We could tell others the Good News: Jesus is risen from the dead.

Some early editors of this Gospel wanted a different ending. They wrote what follows.

JESUS APPEARS TO HIS DISCIPLES [MK.16:9–20]

⁹ That first morning of the week, after he'd risen, he appeared to Mary Magdalene, whose seven demons he'd cast out. ¹⁰ She then went to tell those who'd been with him, who were grieving and tearful. ¹¹ They didn't believe her. He was alive? She'd seen him? ¹² He appeared in a different way to two followers who'd left the city. ¹³ When they reported the appearance, the group didn't believe them either. ¹⁴ Later, he appeared as the eleven reclined at table. He rebuked their unbelief—their hard hearts—because they hadn't believed those who saw him after he'd been raised. ¹⁵ He told them, "Go through the whole world. Preach the Good News to all. ¹⁶ Believers who are baptized will be saved. The unbelieving will be condemned. ¹⁷ Believers will give signs: casting out demons in my name, speaking new tongues. ¹⁸ Without harm they'll touch snakes, without hurt they'll drink poison. They'll lay hands on the sick and they'll be well." ¹⁹ After the Lord Jesus spoke, he was taken up to heaven, where he took his seat at God's right hand. ²⁰ They preached everywhere. The Lord affirmed his word in them with signs.

⸺◈⸺

The author of this section says that, after Jesus appeared to Mary Magdalene, she fulfilled her mission (see 16:7). That she'd been freed from demons reminds us that life is about letting God make us whole. Although Mark described her and two other women allowing fear to keep them from doing what had been asked (see 16:8), the author of this addition suggests that Jesus' appearance freed her to let God's work be done [vv.9–10]. But we hear that Mary's healing mission failed; the disciples weren't consoled [v.11]. The author next tells about an appearance that's described in more detail in the Gospel according to Luke (Lk.24:13–35); and he adds the fact that the returning disciples met the same unbelief that greeted Mary [vv.12–13].

In describing a third appearance, the author notes that the remaining eleven apostles—the disciples closest to Jesus—also refused to believe reports of the resurrection. Jesus' response to their unbelief is remarkable. Immediately after chastising them for hardheartedness, he sends these poor students of the Good News to preach it [vv.14–15]. And he tells them that believers who are baptized will find freedom from all that bedevils them (see 1:13b), whereas unbelievers would be condemning themselves to living in dread [v.16]. He said believers would free others from demons, would speak in new ways, would never know real harm, and would heal [vv.17–18]. Then, says the author, Jesus was no longer seen, but took his place with the Father [v.19]. The hard-hearted disciples obviously reconciled themselves to the Father's plans; they accepted the mission Jesus had given them, and they found the Lord was indeed working in them [v.20].

Index

About the Author

Paul J. McCarren, SJ, works at Loyola Retreat House and at St. Ignatius Church, both in Maryland, while continuing to write Simple Guides to the Bible. A Jesuit priest, he has spent many years in both parish and campus ministry.